Real Stories
Real Teens

Stories by Teens About Making Choices and Keeping It Real

By Youth Communication

Edited by Keith Hefner

YOUTH
COMMUNICATION
True Stories by Teens

Real Stories, Real Teens

Executive Editor
Keith Hefner

Contributing Editors
Rachel Blustain, Loretta Chan, Al Desetta, Andrea Estepa, Katia Hetter,
Phil Kay, Carol Kelly, Nora McCarthy, Tamar Rothenberg, Robin Shulman
and Hope Vanderberg

Layout & Design
Jeff Faerber and Efrain Reyes

Cover Art
Emily Dinan

For reprint information, please contact Youth Communication.

Chapters from *The Bully*, *Summer of Secrets* and *The Fallen*,
of the Bluford Series reprinted with permission
from Townsend Press. (www.townsendpress.com)
Copyright © Towsend Press

ISBN 978-1-933939-70-4

First Edition
Printed in the United States of America

Youth Communication ®
224 W. 29th St., 2nd fl.
New York, NY 10001
212-279-0708
www.youthcomm.org

Dedication

To the teens in the after school programs
at Queens Community House (JHS 217)
and The Center for Family Life (PS 314).

Table of Contents

Contents

Contents

REAL LIFE
Making Connections

My School Is Like a Family

By T. Shawn Welcome

1.   I used to go to a big high school in the Bronx (which I'll call Harding HS, to protect the guilty) and I hated it. It was cold and unfeeling—as close to being put in an institution as I ever want to get. The teachers only cared about the work; it seemed they could care less about any problems a student might be dealing with.

      The students weren't much better. They were there to show off and try to be cool. I was dealing with many personal problems at the time. Going to a big, impersonal school, with metal detectors, I.D. scanners, and hall passes, wasn't helping me at all.

      I started getting more and more depressed and began to cut classes. At one point, I stopped going to school altogether.

      Meanwhile, my guidance counselor was trying to talk me into applying to a small alternative high school called University Heights. She said it was a school that would allow me to work at my own pace and I wouldn't be as stressed as I was at Harding. She kept talking about how the teachers and students were on a first-name basis, and that they had a class called "Family Group," where people would talk to each other about their problems.

      It sounded good but I didn't feel like adjusting to a new school, new people, and a whole load of new work.

2. Taking the Plunge

      She tried to get me to apply there for about a year, but I wasn't budging. Then, in the 11th grade, I heard that my best friend, Eric, had applied and was accepted. He would tell me how free the atmosphere was and how good some of the girls looked. I asked him to pick up an application for me. With my counselor's help,

I filled it out.

It took a couple of visits and a lot of hard work to get in. I had to spend a day there and basically be interrogated by the other students, who play an important part in deciding who is and who isn't right for the school. After that they still didn't want to let me in because I had too many credits to transfer, but my counselor kept calling and pleading with them. In the end, I was accepted.

It was a relief to know that I was finally going to get away from Harding and be able to start a new life. I wanted to leave all my personal and scholastic problems behind. Leaving Harding symbolized the beginning of a new era for me.

All the new students had to go to an orientation during the summer where we played a bunch of get-to-know-each-other games. So, by the first day of school we already knew each other. And University Heights has fewer than 400 students (Harding has about 3,500), so everyone gets to know each other quickly anyway.

> I was dealing with many personal problems at the time. Going to a big, impersonal school, with metal detectors, I.D. scanners, and hall passes, wasn't helping me at all.

My first month at University Heights wasn't what I'd expected. When I heard the word "alternative," I thought that there would be a lot of people who were put there because they had a record of fighting or who had been expelled from other schools. It wasn't like that.

I felt at home there almost right away. I was finally getting what I didn't have at Harding—a feeling that I belonged. At University Heights there wasn't that much fronting going on. I found myself talking to other students about my personal life and taking their advice.

3. **Mutual Support**

Once when we were in class I was talking about the problems I was having with my father. Suddenly I got very emotional. I got up and left the room so the others wouldn't see me cry. Qwana, another student who didn't even know me very well, came out into the hall and held me. I never experienced anything like that at Harding. I don't think anyone did. I didn't even know it was possible.

I didn't know there were other ways of teaching either. For one thing, the classes are not overcrowded. And the teachers don't just write on the blackboard and have you copy the notes.

In Spanish class, for example, the learning is interactive. Frank, one of my Spanish teachers, would write the verbs that we were learning that week on the blackboard and then break the class up into groups of four or five. Each group would have to work together to make sentences with the verbs and the adjectives that we had studied the week before. Then we'd have a contest to see which group made the best sentences. It made me forget I was in class and helped me get to know my peers better.

4. **Teachers Who Care**

The teachers at University Heights are good people too. They have the rare ability to care about their students' lives while still doing their job. Michelle teaches Family Group, which is kind of like homeroom. She understands that students sometimes have problems and she tries to help as much as she can, but she also knows how to get under your skin until you do things right.

My friend Sean would miss some days of school and Michelle would nag him to make up his work. After he spoke to her and she understood that he had financial problems, she helped him get a job in the school. That way she was able to keep an eye on him and he could make some money. Sometimes she gets on our nerves with the nagging, but the people who love you will always annoy you once in a while.

Gus, who teaches gym, is another teacher who's really cool. He always seemed like he was a friend more than a teacher. He would go out of his way to help me with my work and he used to lift weights and play basketball and volleyball with us. Every time I see him now, he's always calling me the future writer. He's always saying that he's going to see me on television reporting the news some day. Gus makes me feel good to be who I am.

5. **Students Who Count**

I always feel respected and cared for by my teachers at University Heights. If I don't, I'll tell them and we'll resolve it. I remember when Marion, one of my teachers, interrupted me when I was talking one time in class. I didn't say anything to her but she could tell that I was upset. She approached me in the hallway and said that she didn't mean to cut me off, but time was running out. I accepted her apology. To tell you the truth, I was shocked that she took the time to apologize to a student.

Now that I'm about to graduate from University Heights I realize that many things about it have helped to make me a better person. Number one is that I always feel like I'm important there. The teachers care about me and not just the work I do. Knowing that has made a big difference in the amount of effort I put into my work and in my feelings about myself and my future.

I left Harding an extremely insecure, scared, confused teenager who wasn't sure what I'd be doing with my life. But, with the presence of caring teachers and friends and as many memories as a person could hope to get in a single year, I've changed. I'm leaving University Heights an ambitious, more intelligent, secure, and decisive man who knows that my only limits are in my imagination.

Bonding Through Cooking

By Aurora Breville

1.   When I entered foster care at age 13, I didn't know how to cook. I truly didn't know my way around the kitchen.

My first foster home was cool because it was just girls living there. That meant not waking up to a raised toilet seat. It also meant being understood. I couldn't picture myself talking to a couple of guys about how my heart got broken on a date, while making a casserole with an apron on.

So, at the same time I got my first taste of cooking, I was able to share my thoughts and feelings and bond with girls my age.

2. **What Is That?**

I remember the day they found out that I couldn't cook. I walked into the kitchen and saw one of the girls making something that wasn't familiar to me: ramen noodles. I stared into the pan, trying hard to see past the foam, and asked in disgust, "What is that?"

The girl gave me a look that said, Are you for real? Then she told me what it was.

Then I asked her, "How do you make that?"

At first she couldn't believe that I asked her how to make ramen noodles. But after a few minutes of stirring the flavor packet into the pan, she told me gruffly, "Get yourself a pan and fill it with water."

Then she said, "Wait for the water to boil and add the noodles. Let it boil for three more minutes and take it off the stove. Are you gonna eat it with the broth?"

I said, "No."

"Then you're gonna need the colander."

"The what?" I asked, perplexed.

"The colander, the strainer, the metal thing with the thousand holes and a handle. You have to use that to drain your noodles." And with that she stalked out of the kitchen with her lunch.

The other girls came strolling into the kitchen soon after she left. One by one they started throwing questions at me.

"Do you know how to make fried chicken?'

"Do you know how to make eggs?"

"Do you know how to clean meat?"

"Do you know how long to fry bacon?"

The idea of cooking for myself was revolting.

As they fired these and other questions at me, I shook my head no. The questions went on and on, and my answer never changed. I honestly expected them to make fun of me and say all sorts of things behind my back, because I was the new girl who didn't know one thing about cooking.

3. Growling Stomach

That was not the case, however, and I'm very glad that I was honest with them. I could've lied about being able to cook, but then I would've made a major mistake like burning the house down, and that wouldn't have been cool.

My next cooking lesson came after the girls heard our foster mother complaining that I was walking around the house grumbling about a growling stomach. I had the nerve to take it a step further and ask my foster mother, "When are you going to cook dinner?"

My foster mother took one look at me and said, "I don't cook for no grown women. I'll cook once in a while, when I feel like it, but otherwise, you go in there and fix yourself something to eat. And close the door on your way out."

I went into the kitchen feeling dejected and hungrier than

ever. I looked through all the cabinets and in the refrigerator. Everything that I saw had to be prepared and cooked in some way, shape, or form. I was ready to give up and go to bed hungry for the first night in my life when "the Cooking Squad" came on the scene.

4. **Cook for Myself?**

"Whatcha doing, Li'l Bit?" Diane asked.

"Just lookin' for somethin' to eat," I said, "that's all."

"You can't be looking for something to eat, chile. You don't have pots and pans out, number one. And number two, you didn't put anything on the counters ready for cooking."

"So what do you want to eat, girl?" Lena asked.

"I don't know yet," I replied, "I'm still trying to decide."

"Why don't you make some macaroni 'n' cheese to go with that chicken left over from yesterday?" Diane suggested.

"Yeah! And you can add some mixed vegetables on the side, you know, to get the vegetable portion out of the way," Kayla offered.

My mind was reeling at this point. I was hungry, and I was going to cook for myself? For real? Get out of here!

I was trying to continue my strict ritual of waiting patiently for someone else to cook for me, something I'd done for 13 years running. Why break such a delightful cycle, I thought. There's nothing wrong with being pampered for one more year. The idea of cooking for myself was revolting. I tried my hardest to get one of the girls to follow through with the food suggestions they made.

5. **First Lesson**

They made me feel like I should've been arrested for asking someone else to cook for me at my age, and concluded by saying something that made me (and my stomach) mad: "I guess you're not all that hungry then."

"Fine!" I snapped. "Then show me how to cook the stupid thing, doggonit!"

Laughing, they told me to get out all the ingredients I needed to make my first dinner: a bowl of leftover chicken, a cup of milk, a pat of butter, the box of macaroni 'n' cheese, and the frozen pack of mixed vegetables.

I don't have to tell you how bad my stomach was growling, but I will. I felt like my stomach was trying to scrape my back! It was hard to concentrate, but I tried following their instructions as much as I could.

I cooked the macaroni first and left it on the stove so that it could stay toasty and warm. I warmed up the chicken in the microwave for three minutes. I did the mixed vegetables last, since they take the least amount of time to cook.

My next cooking lesson involved something that I swore I would never do in my life: cleaning meat. These three girls were determined to change my mind about that and fast!

I woke up one morning to have a bowl of cereal when Diane, the oldest, came into the kitchen. I made a move to leave the kitchen with my bowl when she yelled, "Freeze!"

6. Cleaning Chicken

Of course you know I sat right down and waited for her to bark.

"I gotta teach you how to clean chicken."

Not a "Good morning, did you sleep okay?" Not even a "What's up?" She was determined to get right down to business and didn't care what I thought.

As if on cue, Lena and Kayla came into the kitchen pretending to be sleepy-eyed.

"What are you gonna do with the chicken, Diane?" Kayla asked.

"Nothing. She's gonna clean the chicken for dinner tonight."

Kayla looked at me and looked at Lena and just went to the refrigerator for the milk to go with her cereal. Lena was nice about the whole thing. She came over to where I was sitting and asked, "Have you ever cleaned chicken before?" I shook my head no because my mouth was full of Frosted Flakes.

"It's not hard," she continued. "All you need is a knife and some hot water. Show her, Diane."

"Come over here."

I walked over to the scene of the crime. When I got to the kitchen sink, Diane handed me the knife.

"Pick up the wing and take off the skin with the knife."

I looked at her, looked at the wing, and started to the pull the skin away. When I was finished, I put the wing in the waiting bowl and stared at Diane.

7. **Licking Fingers**

"Do the rest of them," she commanded and walked to the refrigerator.

As I was finishing the rest of the chicken parts, she handed me the lemon.

"Use the lemon to season the meat after you wash it off in hot water. DO NOT use the dishwashing liquid, the hot water's enough."

> **I was not dumb enough to use the dishwashing liquid to wash meat.**

Believe me, I was not dumb enough to use the dishwashing liquid to wash meat. I knew I didn't want to taste any soap on my chicken. Personally, I think she was just saying that to be mean. I thought that everything I was doing was wrong, but when everyone sat down to fried chicken that evening, they were licking their fingers and asking for more. I thought that I was in the clear after that night. Wrong!

My next lesson was to make breakfast for the whole house on cleaning day (Saturday). Diane came into my room at 8:00 in the morning.

"Wake up, Sleepyhead," she said, shaking me. "Come with me to the kitchen. I got something else to teach you."

8. Girlfriend Talk

I gotta tell you that at this point the barking stopped. Diane started talking to me just like any other person. I guess she started having respect for me since I put a hurtin' on that chicken the last time I cooked.

The lessons weren't all bad, either. During the time when I was cleaning the meat, Diane asked all types of questions, like where I lived, what kind of music I liked, and if I went to church. I found out that Diane didn't live too far from me before she came into foster care. We also liked the same kind of music: everything except country and heavy metal.

> When I'm cooking, I sometimes feel like I'm working on something that will help to make a bigger and better me.

This time when Diane took me to the kitchen, Lena and Kayla didn't follow, which was another shock. I guess they figured they wouldn't get any more laughs out of me since I knew (somewhat) what I was doing.

Diane got all the things that I needed to start my first big breakfast: eggs, bacon, sausage, bread, butter, milk, orange juice, and the box of pancake mix.

"Get the big frying pan out of the bottom cabinet."

While I was getting that, she was telling me about the latest episode between her and her boyfriend. While she talked and laughed at all the things that her boyfriend said and did, I prepared the batter and the pan for my pancakes. After the batter was finished, I fried up all the bacon and toasted the bread last, just like she asked.

When I was finished, I felt proud. My taste buds and stomach were pretty happy with what I did, too. It made my heart feel good to see Kayla, the heartiest eater of the house, ask me, "Can you show me how you made your pancakes so golden brown? Mine always come out looking funny and sick!"

When I was alone that evening and every other evening after that, I couldn't help but puff up with pride. It actually felt good knowing that there were dishes out there that were no longer a total mystery to me. I felt a little more like an adult because I didn't have to depend on anyone. I always thought that cooking for myself would be such a chore because of my huge appetite, but it really wasn't!

9. **A Better Me**

I felt wonderful whenever it was time to cook because it meant bonding with other girls my age. It was another adventure for me that held many ups and downs, both in and out of the kitchen. When I'm cooking, I sometimes feel like I'm working on something that will help to make a bigger and better me.

I've definitely come a long way from learning how to make macaroni 'n' cheese and I'm no longer queasy inside about cleaning meat. And making friends has become second nature to me because, just like cooking, it's no longer a crazy idea.

When Politics Gets Personal

By Jason Montoya

1.   Everyone in my family except me is a little old-fashioned and conservative. Over the past few years, I've found myself disagreeing with them about lots of things, like religion, homosexuality and the war in Iraq.

When I say what I think, they get angry at me and sometimes we fight. They seem to think I'm intentionally separating myself from them when I disagree, rather than just wanting to express my opinions.

Once in an argument my brother told me, "You disagree with other people just to cause problems and resist their points of view to show your rebelliousness to the family." That attitude makes me feel like my opinions don't matter, that I don't matter.

2. Fighting Over a TV Show

Once at my grandmother's apartment, my aunts, my mother and I were all watching a Spanish soap opera called *Los Teens*. One of the girls on the show had a baby, and at the end of the episode, she left the baby at an adoption agency.

For the next 10 or 15 minutes, all I heard from my aunts and my mom was, "Oh my God, that's just sending the wrong message to girls nowadays," and, "They should have showed her conquering all odds and still keeping her baby and being successful."

After a while I got tired of listening to their points, which sounded more like what they wanted to see, not how the real world is. So I said, "Well, I think it's a good way to end things. It's more realistic."

Then my mother and my aunts started to bombard me with

questions and comments like, "You really think it's better for her to abandon her child than to try to move forward with her?"

3. Mom Takes It Personally

I defended the character's choice, saying that she didn't want the baby and couldn't support it. We argued about that for a while, and then one of my aunts asked sarcastically, "Then you will allow your daughter to have an abortion?"

I said that I would talk to her seriously about it, but "if she still wanted to have an abortion, I wouldn't stand in her way."

Then my mom snapped, "So that's what you think, huh? OK, it's good to know that's how much you appreciate life, family and the efforts your mother has made for you."

I tried to explain myself. It wasn't that I didn't appreciate my mother and all the things she's done for me, but she was comparing herself to someone in a completely different position. (When she had me, she was married and had a steady income.)

I felt guilty because I'd hurt my mother's feelings, but I was also angry that she wouldn't let me disagree with her without making it a personal attack.

4. Speaking Without Fear

Fortunately, I've found a place where I feel free to express myself without fear of being attacked, where I can talk comfortably about topics that cause trouble at home. This place is TREA (Teens for the Racial and Ethnic Awakening), an after-school discussion group.

About a dozen students and two adult advisors get together once a week, usually in a world history classroom. We cover a different topic at each meeting, ranging from serious issues like homophobia, sex and racism to more laid-back and entertaining topics like music and poetry. I've been an active member for the past two years and I started facilitating meetings last school year.

At TREA, we have rules to ensure that people treat each other's opinions and experiences with respect, and everyone follows them. At one meeting, the topic was abortion, and the atmosphere couldn't have been more different than watching *Los Teens* at my grandmother's.

5. Calm, Friendly Debate

Someone said that she wouldn't have an abortion because that would be committing a murder. Someone else politely replied, "It depends on the way you view life—if you think that a few cells can be considered life," and then said that she supports abortion. Other kids joined in the debate, bringing up religion and their parents' views.

The meeting went on as a friendly, calm discussion, even though we were talking about something that can be emotional and personal. I could listen to the two sides and think about what everyone was saying.

> I looked around and saw that people's expressions were kind and welcoming. No one attacked what I said.

Although I didn't offer my own views at that particular meeting, I've contributed to other discussions and felt valued and at ease.

Instead of getting caught up in an emotional battle like I do at home, I can concentrate on other people's points. Sometimes I've changed my opinions; other times I've learned new ways to explain and defend my views so that other people understand me.

6. More Love Means More Arguing

I've realized why there's such a big difference between my family and TREA. At TREA I have no fear of contradicting somebody because I don't have the same bond with them that I have with the people in my family. It doesn't matter personally to the members of TREA if I disagree with them.

And I have no fear of being contradicted at TREA. I have

to admit that sometimes at home I get passionate and angry in discussions with my family because I want them to agree with me and be on my side. My family is important to me, and I love them.

TREA has given me not only a peaceful retreat from my family but also a new perspective on my relationship with them. During a meeting about relationships, I said something I'd never told anyone before. My ears felt like dynamite, my blood seemed to warm more than 20 degrees, and I knew that my face had turned as red as a tomato.

7. Still Close to Mom

"My mom and I have a good relationship," I said. "Sometimes, I feel like she's a really close friend of mine. However, I feel like there are some issues that we wouldn't be able to talk about. I feel that because she's a little traditional and conservative, I can't talk to her as freely as I would want to."

As I talked, I looked around and saw that people's expressions were kind and welcoming. No one attacked what I said. The next person to speak talked about her relationship with her mother. It was a huge relief to express my conflicting feelings about my mother out loud.

Even though we clash on political and social issues, my mom and I are really close in other ways. Every day I tell her what happened at school, what I got on my exams, the funny stuff that happened in gym class, the projects that I have to do, any problems with my teachers.

She pays more attention to me when I say these things than when we argue about political and social issues. She acts very understanding and talks to me and gives me advice without judging me. We don't have any tension between us, and it feels great because I know she supports and respects me.

8. Can't Tell Mom About Depression

But I can't talk to her about some of my deeper feelings. At one TREA meeting, we had a guest speaker from the National Alliance for the Mentally Ill who talked about depression.

I've felt depressed in the past, and I was relieved to hear an adult acknowledge that it happens to teens. Other members of TREA talked about their experiences with depression, and I was comforted to know that I wasn't alone in having this problem sometimes.

Without saying that I'd been depressed at times, I told my mom about the meeting. She just couldn't understand. She said, "Teenagers shouldn't be depressed. It's not like they have the worries or problems that adults face," like bills or taking care of children. I kept trying to convince her, but she wouldn't accept the fact that adolescents do get depressed.

> **Even though I can't tell her everything about my life, I want to hold onto the closeness my mom and I do have.**

I was disappointed and hurt by my mom's reaction. I knew that I wouldn't be able to talk to her about my depression. She's my mother and I want her to help me when I feel sad, not dismiss me as an ungrateful, spoiled kid.

Even though I can't tell her everything about my life, I want to hold onto the closeness my mom and I do have. But the more we fight about things like abortion, the more I feel like I'm hurting her and driving us apart.

9. **Keeping the Peace**

Because I have TREA as a place to express myself fully, for now I'm trying to avoid having arguments with my mom and the rest of my family. I know that if I changed my beliefs to theirs (or pretended that I agreed with them), we'd have much less tension between us. But I can't do that. I won't lie to them, and I won't lie to myself, either.

Instead, when certain topics come up, I stay quiet or change the subject. For instance, if they're talking about the president, I'll bring up something that happened in the family or ask a question about a TV show that my family watches.

But it's hard to stay away from debates with them, especially when someone says something I'm completely against. I hate having to stifle myself.

I hope that as I get older, my family will stop seeing me as a rebellious kid and start to respect me and my ideas. We still might not agree about political and social issues, but maybe we'll be able to exchange our thoughts peacefully, without hurting one another.

Can a Teacher Be a Friend?

By Zeena Bhattacharya

1.   What do you picture when you hear the word "teacher?" Someone standing in front of the classroom scribbling notes on the board or giving lectures? Is there anything wrong with this picture? Talking to many students, I've gotten the feeling that they'd like to change it. They say they want to break down the barriers created by this system and have more personal, one-on-one relationships with teachers inside and outside the classroom.

Some of the qualities students say they value most in their teachers are flexibility and compassion. They say they want to be treated as individuals with their own needs and problems. "Teachers need to be on a personal level with their students because otherwise I could just read from a book," says Mark Osgood, 16, a high school junior.

Some teachers agree with that. "Students learn more and teachers teach better if a one-to-one relationship exists," says English teacher Charles Roemer.

2. Teachers Who Go the Extra Mile

Many students say they do better in school when a teacher spends extra time and effort on them. Senior Grace Chu (not her real name), 17, says that her Spanish teacher's constant efforts helped her pass her high school graduation exam. "She made sure I understood what I needed to get ahead," Grace says. "Sometimes she would stay after class."

Junior Edgar Quiroa says a math teacher who sat down with him after class and went over material he didn't understand helped him pass the course. To Edgar, an ideal teacher is someone who "can teach, does his job, and is also a friend to the students."

Senior Maghana Taribagil agrees. She says she feels closer to teachers who take time to talk to her outside of class. "I learned more from them than just their particular subjects. I learned about life," she says.

Teachers who are available outside the classroom may open doors to learning that family or other personal problems might have kept locked. Grace Chu feels that the best thing about some of her teachers is that she can confide in them.

3. **Teachers Who Notice**

"If I don't want to go to my family, a teacher would be the next-best person," Grace says. For example, she was able to talk to her health teacher about an alcoholism problem in her family that was troubling her. "He noticed I was depressed and he was willing to listen."

Charles Roemer, who has taught for 29 years, says the need for more personal teacher-student relationships has grown recently. "I see many more students whose experience outside the classroom has handicapped them, so that they are not able to work to their potentials." He added, "Family and social problems have entered their lives when children shouldn't have to deal with these things."

Joel Barsky, a teacher at a small high school, also thinks it's important to have individual relationships with his students. "I stay after class, late in the afternoon," he explained. "I show my students that each one is important to me."

Students also feel that teachers need to be flexible when personal problems affect their ability to do their work. Sarah Popkin, 17, feels grateful to her English teacher for helping her get through a difficult time.

4. **But I Can Explain. . .**

"He knew I was going through a lot of problems, was understanding, and gave assignments to make up my grades," she says.

But Edgar Quiroa complained that his health teacher, who failed him, never listened to students or asked for explanations when they were unable to do the work.

Although most students interviewed said there should be more personal relationships, a few said they can't see themselves opening up to any teacher. "I really don't interact with my teachers," says John Won, 18, a recent graduate. He says that he sees teachers as authority figures and would have a hard time talking "about personal things with people who can affect your grade." He added, "I don't feel comfortable."

> Sometimes, both teachers and students say, concern about grades get in the way of learning and relating to one another.

Grades seem to be the most common reason students give for wanting to keep their distance. Junior Ivo Dimitroff agrees that there should be a line between teachers and students. "I don't think that teachers should be involved in our personal affairs," he says. "Sometimes the grades could be affected, and also the teachers look at the students in a different way."

5. **Breaking Down the Barriers**

Sometimes, both teachers and students say, concerns about grades get in the way of learning and relating to one another. But a bad grade on a math test taught June Lau that her teachers care about more than just her grades. June recalls that she was so worried about her grade that she actually started crying. But her math teacher came to the rescue. "She gave me a big hug and said, 'Just because you got a bad mark on your test, I'm not going to think of any less of you.'"

A number of teachers are trying to get rid of the boundaries that have existed in traditional classrooms. Joel Barsky believes the best way to do this is to arrange students in groups and allow them to choose their own topics.

6. Destroy Big High Schools

"I'm not always going to stand up in front of the classroom and put notes on the board, or ask them to read at home," he says. Barsky believes that getting students to work on their own makes them more responsible. "They begin to ask more questions. They want to learn more for themselves."

Teachers admit that although they would like to give individual attention to every student, it isn't always easy to do, especially in large classes and big schools.

What can be done about this? "Destroy big high schools," suggested Joel Barsky. Charles Roemer, who teaches in a traditional high school, likes the idea of an alternative high school with much smaller classes. "We are starting to move in the right direction with smaller classes," he says.

THE REAL ME
Being Yourself

Running From Myself

By Jennifer R.

1.   The summer after 7th grade, I went to stay with my father. I was so excited because I hadn't seen him for years.

    I arrived there a shy and obedient child, but over the summer I changed into a social and wild adolescent. At first I loved it because, for the first time in my life, I felt included and free. Then things changed.

    My parents separated when I was 1 year old, and I grew up as an only child. I spent most of the day with my grandmother, playing games like cooking show and dolls. When Mom picked me up from Grandma's house, I went home and watched TV until bedtime. That's what Mom did too; she was tired after work.

    Life with Mom was boring. I had no one to play with. Sometimes I'd catch her on a good day, usually on weekends, and we'd bug out together. We'd play music and dance around the house as if we were on Broadway. But other times I made believe I was two people and played games alone.

2. Too Shy to Make Friends

    I didn't have friends in school. I wasn't used to being social. I was too shy to talk to anyone I didn't know. And no one asked me to be their friend. I was the fat, shy, smart girl in class that no one noticed.

    I didn't start out fat, but by the time I was 11 I weighed 180 pounds. I loved Grandma's cooking and could eat plates of it. I ate candy and drank soda, and I didn't play outside. But I hated

---

(All names have been changed.)

being fat and shy.

I dreamed of being cool. I imagined how my life would be different if I were in the "in" crowd. I'd know the good gossip and I'd say "hi" to everyone when I walked down hallways. I envied the attention they got.

3. Daddy Treated Me Like a Princess

I saw my father on occasional weekends, and he paid attention to me. When I was little, he'd swing me around and carry me on his shoulders. We played kiddie games and laughed at silly jokes. He treated me like a princess.

I hated not seeing him every day. I often asked him to get back with Mom, but every time he told me no. By the time I was 5, he was living with his girlfriend Rosa, her two kids, Sandra and Luis, plus the two little kids they had together. I didn't know them well, but I didn't want to because I felt they took my father from me.

> **No one asked me to be their friend. I was the fat, shy, smart girl in class that no one noticed.**

Then my father and I lost contact when Mom and I moved to Staten Island with her fiancé, Stan. At first, I felt like I was missing a part of me.

I didn't ask why Dad wasn't around anymore because I was afraid the answer might be he didn't want to see me, or my mother didn't want me to see him. I told myself that maybe Mom didn't tell him that we moved, or he didn't have the time to see me.

After four years, my mom broke up with Stan, and we moved to Brooklyn. Then my father called that New Year's Eve. I was stunned. Mom told me that she'd been looking for him for the past year.

"When are you going to come see me? I miss you," Daddy said to me. After he talked to Mom, she asked me if I'd like to go to his house for the summer.

I wasn't sure. I worried that maybe I wouldn't be accepted by his family. And now they lived in Pennsylvania, too far to come home if I didn't like it. But he really wanted to see me and I missed him and wanted to make him happy. I finally said, "Yeah, I wanna go."

4. **I Partied and Had Fun**

The summer after 7th grade, I went to Easton, Pennsylvania, where he lived. But I only saw him at night and on weekends because he worked long hours.

To my surprise, I had a lot of fun. I hung out with people. I went to parties with Sandra and Luis, who were a little older than me, and my two cousins, Cara, who was 16, and Adam, 17. They became my buddies.

Being social was a new experience for me. And so was trying drugs like alcohol, marijuana and cigarettes, which I'd never even thought of doing before. I was curious and excited to be experimenting.

My new buddies took me to my first club on my 12th birthday. I had a blast. I hung out, met guys, and afterwards we got wasted on beer and hard liquor.

5. **Finally, I Was Cool—I Thought**

I thought I was cool. I felt like I belonged. Even though I was still heavy, it didn't seem to matter to my buddies. I felt like an adult. No one told me I couldn't do something because I was too young.

Daddy wasn't aware of what we did. He worked all day and came home too late to worry. And when he was suspicious of us smoking, we lied about it. But I think if he'd found out, he'd have been furious.

At the end of the summer, I didn't want to leave. When I got home, I rebelled against Mom for not letting me be free.

6. **Back Home, I Rebelled**

Thinking about it now, I think I rebelled against myself. I was looking for some way not to be the person that I'd left at home. Rebelling wasn't me—and so it was exactly what I wanted. It helped me keep the feeling of being free.

I wanted to be like my father's other kids, loose and wild. My father and Rosa gave them too much freedom. They let them stay out as long as they wanted and they didn't even have to go to school if they didn't want to.

So, when I went to school the first day of 8th grade I decided it would be my last. That was my first step toward being like them. Each day I waited for my mom to go to work. Then, after walking halfway to school, I'd go home and watch TV. Sometimes I cursed a lot at home for no reason, like they would. Sometimes I stole cigarettes from Mom and smoked them in the bathroom like they would.

I wanted to be bad; I felt I needed to be a completely different person from the shy good girl who lived alone with her mom. I felt liberated by not going by the rules. I wanted to see how far my freedom would go and how much I could get away with.

7. **Mom Confronted Me**

But Mom was too smart for me. After two weeks cutting, she confronted me. "Jenny, we need to discuss what's been going on with you lately," she said. "Why have you been acting so strangely?"

"I don't know," I replied. I didn't want to tell her about anything that was going on. I wanted to keep my distance and independence.

She started crying. "Please tell me what you want. Let me know what you're going through. I want to help you get through this." She was heartbroken that I was changing.

But I just stood there quietly; her distress didn't faze me.

"Do you want to go with your father? Will that make you

happy?" she asked.

"Yes," I said, without thought, not caring how hurt my mother was. I just wanted the fun summer experience back.

8. Back to Dad's—But the Fun Ended

So I went back to my father's. He accepted me with open arms, but everyone else was wondering why I came back. "You were lonely over there, weren't you?" Cara asked. I had to admit it.

I was so excited to be back. I hung out like I wanted. I smoked, drank and had my fun. But after six months, my buddies from the summer started to treat me differently. They made fun of my squeaky voice, my non-hip-hop style, my weight, my glasses and my frizzy hair.

> **I felt liberated by not going by the rules.**

I felt like I was thrown into a desert and vultures were surrounding me, waiting for me to let my guard down. I felt alone in a house full of people. It was like I wasn't even part of their family. I was an outcast. To make matters worse, my dad thought we were moving back to Manhattan, and took everyone out of school. But the apartment fell through. We were out of school for nothing, and I was stuck in the house every day with these people.

9. I Got High to Forget

I started to take drinking and smoking pot and cigarettes seriously—and began to depend on them. I kept telling myself that being high would take away the madness. I smoked every day so that I didn't have to recognize when I was being teased.

I called Mom many times to ask her to take me back, but every time she gave me an excuse. She told me that she'd made my room a storage space. I felt like she wanted me gone. I assumed she didn't love me. I felt hurt and unwanted. I felt so alone and depressed.

10. Conversations With Myself

As I sat there alone, I had conversations with myself about what I wished for, what I didn't have, what I didn't do, why I wasn't accepted. I spoke to myself, then cried to myself. I wished I could find love, true friends, a life.

> I needed to break out of my insecure shell. If I didn't try to change, nothing would get better.

I told myself that my former buddies were jerks and didn't like anyone but themselves. I told myself to speak up, to defend myself. But then I thought that it was my destiny to be miserable. I thought I was just going to have to live with it.

After about a year, we finally moved to Manhattan. I was in 8th grade again and started thinking to myself that I needed to make an effort to change. I didn't want to be depressed anymore. I didn't want to be alone anymore. I needed to break out of my insecure shell. If I didn't try to change, nothing would get better.

11. More Social, But Still Me

Then, on the day I started school, I heard some boys rating how cute I was. Some girls introduced themselves to me. "Have I already changed?" I wondered.

I began to feel more social. I became more open by saying more of what was on my mind and not holding back, and people wanted to be my friend. I was surprised by the attention, and happy to have anyone as a friend.

I even started dating. Boys were actually coming up to me to ask me out. Having other people accept me made me feel I could love myself more. But I was still self-conscious about my looks, even though I'd lost a lot of weight. (I guess I'd lost interest in eating when I was feeling down and alone.)

12. I Had to Help Myself

I no longer cared about the parties and the drugs because I didn't need them anymore. And I started to get into my studies again. Knowing that other people liked me for who I was helped me ignore the situation with my cousins and step-siblings at home. It wasn't easy to forget about what they thought of me, but I tried.

I realized that I needed to depend on myself. I got my own job at a clothing store, which I really enjoyed because I was able to be more independent.

At the end of 10th grade, I had a serious talk with my mother. For two years I'd only talked to her on the phone and visited her job. I asked her if I could spend the weekend at her house.

13. A Big Talk With Mom

Once there, I showed her how well I was doing in school. "I'm so proud of you," she said with a big smile on her face. I spoke to her about what I did and why I rebelled. "I needed to have fun," I told her. "I felt like moving was the only way I could get it."

She understood. I also told her how miserable I was living with my father because of the people around him. She listened to every word. I realized how lucky I was with her. I didn't need to rebel. I was just too young in the mind. I didn't know what I was getting myself into.

But after that summer with my mom, going back to my father's was the right move because I would've become so caught up in the fact that my mom wasn't lenient like my dad. I would've lived my days hating Mom for no reason.

14. I Learned My Lesson The Hard Way

Now Mom and I have worked things out. We spend weekends together. I've decided that I want to move back to Brooklyn with her.

I haven't told Daddy yet because I think it's best to take it slow with him. My father's said he wants to be with me more than ever. He's a sweet and caring man, and the last thing I want to do is break his heart. But now that I have the maturity to make better decisions, I need to do what's best for me.

A Short Cut to Independence

By Anita Chikkatur

1.   For years, I needed my mom's help to twist my long, thick hair, which fell nearly halfway down my back, into a braid or even a ponytail. I hated doing that every morning because it made me feel helpless. I hated the long hours it took to wash and dry my hair.

I wanted to feel free and independent. I wanted a haircut. But I couldn't make myself do it. A haircut was a big decision. My hair was more than just hair. It was a symbol of control.

I held back for a year because I was afraid of what my parents would say. The last time I cut it was when I was 10 and first came to America. For my parents and relatives, long hair is part of being a woman. Especially for "good Indian girls."

Most of my friends didn't want me to go short, either. I'm not sure why. Maybe they were like me, afraid of change. Somewhere inside, I believed that the really beautiful women had long hair. I remembered someone saying that college guys liked women with long hair. (And college is the place where you meet your husband.)

But my friend Hee Won told me that it didn't matter what people would say. Finally, last May, I decided to do it.

2. Getting the Cut

I chose the day before a school break because I didn't want friends seeing me with short hair before I got used to it. Hee Won agreed to go with me because I probably would have chickened out if she didn't.

We walked around my neighborhood, trying to find a good but

cheap salon. I almost hoped we wouldn't succeed. My stomach hurt. (Do 16-year-olds get ulcers?) But we did. It said, "$10 for cut, any length."

When we went inside, Hee Won and I looked through a magazine for a style. I found a model with a really cropped cut and showed the haircutter.

The stylist put a white sheet around me. I took a deep breath, trying to relax. He sprayed water on my hair. I talked nervously to Hee Won. Then he started cutting.

> Cutting my hair was my way of rebelling against my parents, but I didn't realize that cutting it was only half the struggle.

The worst part was the crunchy sound when he chopped off the first six inches of my hair. I thought that maybe I should tell him not to go any further.

I could see my hair all around me on the floor. (And at any moment, my lunch might have joined it.) I guess my nervousness showed because the haircutter smiled and said, "You won't be needing that anymore." Easy for him to say. He and Hee Won were casually singing along to the radio, while I was scared to death.

For the next part, he told me to take my glasses off. I'm half-blind so I couldn't even see myself in the mirror, let alone what he was doing. But I took my glasses off anyway. I had decided I should go all the way. Besides, how short could it be?

When I put my glasses back on, it was over. Too late to change my mind.

3. **Panic Time**

My hair was so short that some of it was sticking up. The stylist told me that was because my hair had to get used to being that short.

Forget the hair, what about my parents? Panic time. Hee Won

told me it looked great. I just nodded and paid my $10.

I walked outside and immediately felt that everyone was staring at me. It's because you look great, I told myself. Yeah, right. It looked horrible, I wasn't meant to have short hair, it will never grow back, my parents will kill me.

We stopped at a store to buy a Knicks hat. It was partly to cover my new haircut and partly because I had always wanted one, but hats and my long hair wouldn't cooperate. Now, the hat fit perfectly.

Cutting my hair was my way of rebelling against my parents, but I didn't realize that cutting it was only half the struggle. Now I had to go home and face them.

4. My Parents React

When I walked in my dad was on the phone. "What happened?" he said.

"I got a haircut," I said, trying not to sound nervous. He was silent so I went to my room. I listened to the radio and paced. I stared at myself in the mirror, trying to get used to the new me.

When my mom walked in, I was reading. She stared for a moment. "I don't like it one bit," she said. "It screws up your whole face."

I pretended to ignore her. I wasn't hoping for an, "It looks great...I'm glad you did it," but I wasn't expecting anything that cruel. I told my friends that since she didn't like it, I probably looked great. I was lying, of course.

At least my dad didn't say anything, I thought. Then I overheard him talking about my "awful haircut." Later that night, my mom told me that he yelled at her for "letting" me cut my hair.

5. Facing Friends and Family

My friends' reactions were more diverse, ranging from "I couldn't recognize you from the back!" to "You should be in *Vogue* modeling that haircut." A close friend, who is Indian and had hair almost down to her waist, wasn't thrilled, but she said she "was getting used to it."

Another friend said, "You look like a lesbian." Oh really? I didn't know cutting your hair meant changing your sexual preference.

Five days after my haircut, I went to New Orleans to visit my relatives. What would they say?

My aunt freaked. "I can't believe you cut your hair," she said, turning to my uncle. "She had such pretty hair." I still did. "I can't believe you cut your hair. You had such pretty hair..." Okay, I got your point already.

> I overheard my dad talking about my 'awful hair cut.'

This was how my uncle introduced me to a guest at his house: "This is my nephew...uh...I mean niece," he said. Ha, ha.

It got better. "She had long hair before," he explained. "I guess she hates to be beautiful."

I became convinced that the haircut was a huge mistake. I tried to tell myself that it didn't matter what my relatives thought. But I was really hurt by their comments.

Back in New York, I told anyone who would listen what my relatives had said. My friends said that they were just jerks.

6. My New Hair Fit My Lifestyle

It took me about two weeks to get used to the cut and a month to realize short hair was right for me. When I was younger I always wore my hair the way my mom wanted it. This time, I'll keep it short because I like the way I look.

Needing my mom's help to style my hair made me feel young and helpless. But now, I can style it myself. It is fun to run my hands through my hair and not worry about getting it tangled. It feels great to wash and dry my hair in less than 15 minutes.

I'm also the kind of person who feels more comfortable in jeans and T-shirts than in dresses, so my new no-fuss hairstyle fits my lifestyle.

Friends tell me I look older with short hair. Better yet, I feel older and more secure about myself. In spite of the reactions of my parents and my relatives I'm glad I cut my hair.

I'm Black, He's Puerto Rican. So What?

By Artiqua Steed

1.   One day I was walking down the street with my best friend and my sister when this guy rode by us on a bike. I noticed him right away. He had a caramel-colored complexion, and very pretty eyes, kind of like my father.

    I told my friend that I thought he was cute. So she turned around and called him. "Hey, hey you, on the bike," she said. He turned around. "Yeah, you, come here," she said. "My friend wants to talk to you." I was very embarrassed. I couldn't believe she had actually done that.

    But it worked. The guy started to come back toward us. I had thought he was a light-skinned black, but I saw as he came closer that he was Latino. I thought to myself, "It must be really dark out here for me not to have noticed before that he's Puerto Rican." But since he was cute I didn't really care.

2. **Not What I Expected**

    I was very nervous. I didn't even ask him his name. All I could say was hi. He asked me my name and how old I was. We talked for a few minutes and then he asked me for my number. I didn't want to give it to a guy I didn't know, but I took his.

    When he gave me the paper I looked down at it and it said Johnny. "Johnny," I thought, "What kind of name is that?" It was so plain. I'm used to unusual names. Besides, I thought he would have a Hispanic name.

    He told me to call him the next day at 3 p.m. After I walked away from him I had a huge grin on my face. When I finally caught up to my sister and my friend, they started laughing at me. But I didn't mind.

3. 'Yes, I'll Go Out with You'

I called Johnny the next day at around 3 o'clock, like he said. The phone rang and then a recording came on. I was mad. How could he tell me to call and then not be there? I called him back about 20 minutes later. This time he answered.

We talked for two hours about everything. He told me about himself and the things he liked to do. He told me that he was a DJ and also wrote songs.

After three days of talking on the phone, we finally decided to see each other again. We had a nice time even though we only went to his house. He made a compilation of all of my favorite songs. We spoke to each other every day after that. After three or four weeks, he asked me to go out with him. I said yes before he could finish his sentence.

4. Was I Dissing Black Men?

I didn't know what I was getting myself into—him being Puerto Rican and me being black. I'd never had an inter-racial relationship before, and it caught me by surprise!

I thought it would be different to date someone who was not black.

I'd thought about the issue of dating someone of another race, but could never imagine myself doing it. I was always very into black pride and thought that any black man who thought another woman was more beautiful than a black woman was crazy.

And I strongly believed that a black woman who dated a man of another race was ignoring how hard black men had to work to get where they are.

But when I met Johnny my attitude started to change. I still have pride in my race, but I came to realize that if a black woman dates a man of another race, it doesn't mean that she's given up on black men. And thinking that black women are more beautiful than women of any other race is just going overboard.

I have to admit that the fact that Johnny is not black is one of the reasons why I started liking him so much. I thought it would be different to date someone who was not black. I was excited to learn more about him and his background, culture and beliefs. I wanted to see the world from his perspective. I even found myself trying to learn Spanish.

5. My Sister Is a Bigot

At first, it was hard to look at him and not see his color. But, as I got to know him, I found Johnny to be no different than any black guy I have known, except for the fact that he's Puerto Rican and speaks Spanish.

Not everyone saw it that way. My brother and sister and even some of my friends gave me a hard time for going out with Johnny. When I called him, my brother would say things like, "Are you on the phone with that rice-and-bean-eating Puerto Rican?"

My sister was even worse. She is what you would call a bigot. She feels that there is no need for anyone in her family to be dating someone who is not black.

My best friend once asked my sister, "What would you do if I married a white man?" My sister's exact words were, "Don't bring him to my house." She once told me that she didn't like Johnny and I know it's because he's not black.

6. My Own Stereotypes

I have to admit that when Johnny and I first started going out, it was hard for me to get past my own stereotypes about Puerto Ricans. I thought they had no color coordination (my sister always said that they were the ones who came outside with mismatched colors and no socks), that all they liked to eat was rice and beans and that they were always copying black fashions and music.

Before meeting Johnny, I often found myself having conversations that were critical of Latinos. I remember one time when my sister and I saw a Puerto Rican couple fighting on the street. The guy was hitting the girl. I said to my sister that if the girl had been black, she would have fought back. My sister agreed with me. I never considered that the girl was just scared of her boyfriend and that's why she let him hit her.

7. 'That's My Boyfriend You're Talking About'

Now when I hear racial slurs against Puerto Ricans, I am offended by them, because I've learned that they are not true. It hurts me when people dis Puerto Ricans because they are talking about my boyfriend.

Whenever my friends and family do it, it makes me feel bad because they don't see that they are talking about someone I care a lot about. The other day, I snapped at my sister for saying something stupid about Puerto Ricans. I don't remember what she said but I know it made me mad.

Johnny's family has never said anything against me or our relationship as far as I know. Some of his friends even told him they thought I was pretty and asked him if I had any friends for them. He does have one friend who doesn't like

> **It hurts me when people dis Puerto Ricans because they are talking about my boyfriend.**

morenas, (a Spanish name for dark-skinned girls), but I've never met the guy and he hasn't done anything to come between us.

Johnny and I have been going out for several months now and we get along fine considering the racial difference. I feel that he respects me more than any other guy I have dated. This doesn't have anything to do with the fact that he is not black; it's just the type of person he is.

The hard part is dealing with other people's attitudes. Interracial dating is still hard for a lot of folks to accept. But if two people are in love or like each other a lot, then racial or ethnic differences will not wreck the relationship.

I've Been an Adult Too Long: I Need Time to Be a Teen

By Marlene Peralta

1.   Last year when I finished high school, I wanted to go away to college. I thought it would be the best thing for my future. I'd be by myself, learning to be independent, and I wouldn't have all the interruptions I usually have at home, so it would be easy for me to study for exams.

    But when I told my mother that I wanted to go away, she said she needed me to stay with her to take care of my 8-year-old brother and 1-year-old sister.

    When my mother told me this, I said to her, "You are selfish, because you know that if I stay here, it will not be easy for me to study."

    But she said, "The selfish one is you because you know that I have a lot of responsibilities and I can't handle them without you."

    After the conversation ended, I almost cried.

2. ## Too Many Missed Opportunities

    All through high school, I missed out on a lot of opportunities because I had to take care of my brother and sister. I couldn't be part of the volleyball team at my school, even though I've played volleyball all my life, because I had to pick up my brother after school.

    I also wanted to be part of a Hispanic club called Aspira, but I couldn't go because I had to be at home looking after my brother and sister while my mother was at work.

    It always seemed unfair to me when my mother would go to

the mall or somewhere else where she could take my little sister with her but chose not to. Instead, my mother made me stay in the house to take care of her.

When I thought about all the things like that that had happened in high school, and about the fact that they might happen all over again in college, I wanted to cry.

I felt like my mother didn't care about my future.

3. Am I Selfish for Wanting to Leave Home?

But even though I felt angry, I also felt selfish for wanting to go away. When my stepfather heard me and my mother arguing, he told me that my mother was reacting that way because she hated to think of me living away from her.

I have a good relationship with my mother; I tell her all the things that happen to me, even about guys. She gives me advice about how to deal with life. So part of the reason she probably wants me to stay is that we are so close.

And when my mother first came to the United States, she came alone and we didn't see each other for five years.

Living with my grandparents for those five years made me more independent. But I think my mother fears being without me all over again.

4. My Mother Needs My Help

And it's true that my mother has many responsibilities. My mother works as a home attendant taking care of an old lady. She works long hours to earn enough money to support us and to save money because she is trying to bring my grandparents to this country.

The days when I can't look after my brother and sister are hard for her. She has to ask for permission from her job to pick up my brother at school, and she has to rush there and back.

After work, she usually cooks dinner and bathes my sister at the same time, which makes her frantic. And then she doesn't get to rest until after dinner, when she's finished washing the dishes.

My mother was a 7th-grade teacher when she lived in the Dominican Republic. She regrets having come to this country because she says that here she is making a lot of sacrifices, getting old without getting any rest.

Seeing the hard work that my mother has to do makes me realize that she really does need help. Though I had responsibilities when I was younger, I also had a lot more free time than I do now.

5. I Want to Dance, Play Volleyball, Learn the Guitar

I was on both the school volleyball team and the neighborhood volleyball team. I participated in a teen discussion group at my church. We also had trips to the beach or rivers and parties celebrating birthdays or Christmas.

These things made me happy and they helped me have many friends.

Now I would like to continue doing the things I already know how to do, like dance and play volleyball. I would also like to learn to play the guitar. But I'm stuck at home. I think I have a good mother because she cares about me.

Right now she is trying to work fewer hours to free me of the responsibilities at home. She wants me to take the time I need to work hard in college. But I feel like leaving home is the only possible way for me to escape from these responsibilities.

It is important to me to be responsible and help my family, but it is also important to do what I need to feel good about myself.

6. I'm a Teenager—I Need to Have Fun

Going away to college will help me to be more independent and to be able to make my own decisions about my future.

I have to begin thinking about myself, and not just in terms of schoolwork; I am young and I need to have fun now. I need to play my real role, which is to be a teenager, because for too long, I have been playing the role of an adult.

Princess Oreo Speaks Out

By Dwan "Telly" Carter

1. "You're just weird."

   "If I wasn't looking at chu, I'd have thought you was white."

   "Say that again, you said that mad white."

   I often get comments like that from classmates, friends and even my family. Sometimes I laugh back, but the comments also hurt my feelings. I know they don't mean anything by it, but I don't really like that they think I'm so strange.

   I'm a dark-skinned female, a descendent of Africans. I grew up in a black family in a largely black neighborhood, and I'm conscious of the disadvantages that have plagued African-Americans for generations. So what's the deal?

   It seems that, for a lot of people around me, being black is an attitude. According to my peers, if you're black, you listen to hip-hop, r&b and reggae.

   The ability to dance is a given, and of course, you know how to do dances like the bank-head bounce and wining. You eat Caribbean foods and Southern-style cooking, and if you're female, you know about head wraps and weaves.

2. **Dad Taught Me Pride**

   Anything else and it's like you're from another planet, or at least that's how I feel. I do a lot of things that people around me don't associate with being black. My friends laugh at me because I'd rather listen to Limp Bizkit than Jay-Z. They love to tease me about watching *Dawson's Creek* and *Felicity*.

   It doesn't seem to matter that I watch *Moesha* and *The Parkers* too. Because of my tastes and the way I talk (I use big vocabulary words), people jokingly call me "Oreo": black on the outside, white on the inside.

But to me, being African-American means my skin color shows a history of enslavement and discrimination. Knowing my history and understanding where I come from is very important to me. It's what keeps me grounded and focused on taking advantage of the opportunities that African-Americans fought for.

My dad instilled that knowledge and pride in me. As African-Americans, he says, we should be in debt to those who risked their lives to give us the opportunities we have, particularly education. His understanding of being black has a lot to do with our history and our future.

> People jokingly call me 'Oreo': black on the outside, white on the inside.

But for my peers, being black has more to do with fitting into the culture right here and now. They make me feel like I'm not black enough. And they tease me even more when I try to show them that I can be (their version of) black.

3. I Sound Like a Fool

When I try to be down with the slang and fit in, half the time I end up sounding like a fool.

"I-ight peace yo."

"You's a Doga man."

"Peace out boo-boo."

It just doesn't come out right. The words get all jumbled and tumble out wrong, and my friends look at me as if I've spoken to them in another language. All my efforts end in giggles (I'm laughing at myself right now) or in gut-busting laughter with tears streaming down my friends' faces.

My friends tease me even worse when I try to show them that I can dance to reggae, calypso and hip-hop. It just doesn't work well. I'd never get invited to *Soul Train* (a popular black dance party on TV in the 1980s.) My style is more like Soul-less Train.

4. A Duck With Seizures

It's not just friends who paint me "white." One time, my sister and I were reciting some lyrics from "You're All I Need," by Method Man featuring Mary J. Blige. My sister was reciting the rap lyrics and I was singing the hook. I was trying to be just like Mary—the bounce in her movements, the way she moved her neck, her hand motions, everything.

I was so into the song, I forgot my sister was in the room with me. I thought I was doing well until my sister's hard laughter broke my concentration. She was doubled over with tears streaming out of her eyes. She was laughing so hard she couldn't talk, and her hand was motioning for me to stop.

Then through bits of dying laughter, she said, "Stop...stop trying to act ghetto, girl, you making my sides hurt." She said I looked like a duck having seizures.

Maybe I didn't move right? Since I'm African-American, I should have some rhythm, huh? And I should be able to mimic Mary?

I didn't let it show, but it hurt that even my own sister didn't see me as black enough.

5. Am I Lacking Something?

What bothers me about being called white—besides the fact that I'm not—is that it seems I must be lacking something and I'm not sure what it is.

My friend told me once, "Maybe one day you'll wake up and become Dawnesha." At the time, I was a geeky freshman in high school, insecure about who I was. I wondered if I could transform myself into someone my peers would recognize as a true black girl.

I'd have loved to put on those big hoop earrings I saw my friends wearing. I'd be wearing snake-patterned denim outfits, popping my gum, and showing off a nameplate that said

REAL STORIES, REAL TEENS

"Dawnesha." My hair would be dyed, fried and laid to the side. And I'd rank on somebody with those fluid motions of the neck and hand that make the "African-American girl" infamous.

Sigh. I would've loved it. I just wanted to fit in.

6. No Stereotype for Me

Then reality knocked some sense into me. I didn't have enough attitude to pull that off. And it just wasn't me.

Besides, Dawnesha would be as much of a stereotype as the *MADtv* character Bunifa. Played by Debra Wilson, Bunifa has a fierce attitude, big mouth and snaps on anyone. Her clothes are tight, she always has her hair done and she gives her homegirl a "shout out" no matter where she is.

While Debra Wilson is funny, and Bunifa does ring true in some ways, the character makes me a little angry. She's ignorant about the things around her and she always starts arguments for no reason. That's not someone I'd want to be like.

It's one thing to fit in, but my trying to be Dawnesha would've been like acting out a stereotyped role.

Now, as I reach my final semester of my senior year, I'm more aware of myself, who I am, and who I want to be: me. Even saying "Dawnesha" makes me feel weird. That's not who I am. Dwan is my name and I'm comfortable with that. Being different makes me unique. I even gave myself a nickname, "Princess Oreo" (though my dad hates it).

7. What About Chuck Berry?

I'm getting used to people staring at me when they hear me blasting rock music. I think it makes them feel uncomfortable because they're not used to an African-American girl bobbing her head along to rock and roll music.

"Hey," I want to tell them, "music is music." Besides, rock music was developed by black artists like Little Richard and Chuck Berry well before acts like the Beatles came along.

And there's a lot of crossover in music. There's a thin line between musical categories nowadays, and a lot of overlap in musical audiences. Plenty of white kids listen to hip-hop. And I know I'm not the only person of color who knows the lyrics to songs by popular white artists.

My reading tastes are diverse, too. I like to read books by white authors, such as Isaac Asimov and Tami Hoag, as well as by black authors, like Octavia Butler, Toni Morrison and Malcolm X. Maybe it's because I read a lot that I talk the way I do.

8. **Playing My Air Guitar**

It's not that I'm purposely acting white—it's not even a thought that crosses my mind. I just like what I like, and I don't know why other people can't be more open-minded.

Even though my dad emphasizes the heritage aspect of being African-American, he's not above making the same cultural assumptions as my friends. One evening, as my family and I were sitting around the dinner table, I turned on a rock station and started dancing to a song by a Canadian rock band. Everyone stopped eating and gawked at me (I thought they'd be used to me by now), trying to hold back laughter.

> **When I try to be down with the slang and fit in, half the time I end up sounding like a fool.**

But even when the laughter came, I kept on dancing. My dad said, "It's too late for you, girl." I knew he meant I was hopelessly white. I smiled and started to do my lame air guitar. I didn't care what they thought about me. I was happy. And that was my song.

REAL FRIENDS
The Meaning of Friendship

The Fantastic Four: My Friends and I Are Tight

By Stephen Simpson

1.   Any given day…the phone rings…
"Hello?"
"Yo, what's up, Stephen?"
"Nothin'. What we doing today?"
"We meetin' at Eric's house at 1:00. Call Leon."
"OK. Head over here, I should be dressed by then."
"All right, peace."
"Peace."
Click. Just a typical day being planned out by me and my boys: Ivan Jackson, Eric Wright and Leon Quick. This is what we do.

    When we get together, anything can happen. Whether it's spending the day having Wrestlemania XX, going from court to court ballin' or staying home playing video games and talking, we do it.

    Whenever one of us is doing something, we try to get the others involved. I feel good when I'm with my friends because we keep each other happy. We stick together, and I think that's important because if you don't have your friends, who do you have?

    When we are around each other, it doesn't matter what we think or say. Sometimes we let it all hang out.

2. **Three Amigos**

    Our togetherness has given us many titles by many people.

    Back when Leon didn't hang out with us too much, people started calling us the Three Stooges (we don't answer to that), the Three Musketeers or the Three Amigos.

I consider us to be like the old A-Team: we have a smart guy, a silly guy, a strong guy, and a good leader.

Eric is the "brawn"—the strong guy—of our outfit. He's the biggest (in weight), but also the youngest (14). He's always trying to fight one of us for no particular reason. Eric's cockiness often causes other problems apart from our group. (We've just barely avoided two or three fights.)

Some good things about Eric are his "get up and go" spirit, (which usually lasts around five minutes tops), his helpfulness, because he tries to help if he can, and his generosity (sometimes).

3. **Covering for Each Other**

Ivan is the silly guy in our group without a doubt. He will almost always "dumb out" in any given situation, with one of us having to bail him out.

When he tried to date two girls at the same time, I had to cover for him (as usual). Both girls wanted to dump him, but with a lot of persuasion (and some begging) from yours truly, they eventually forgave him (and one went out with him).

We usually end up laughing at the ridiculous jams Ivan puts himself in. But I like his "get everyone involved" mentality and his sense of humor. He tries to be the clown and he'll laugh at anything, even jokes on him.

Leon is the leader of the group. We try to listen to him because he is the oldest (22), and because he makes the right call in most situations.

We all have our shining moment as leader, but Leon's age and his "pick up the slack" attitude make him the permanent one. He tells us if we're falling off, and he picks us up with his cheerful disposition.

4. **Flexing My Muscles of Knowledge**

As for me, I believe that I am the smart guy in the group (Eric and Ivan might argue). I try to flex my muscles of knowledge.

Sometimes when we pick something to do, I try to sort out every possible thing that might happen, or I advise my friends not to make certain choices by explaining the consequences.

They say I try to make everything perfect or neat. I'm always tucking something in or fixing something sloppy. I try to use full vision—focusing on things that could happen in the long run. And with my fast-talk negotiator methods, sometimes I can talk people into giving or helping us with things (they always send me to do that).

I also try to keep us from getting in trouble (it doesn't always work). My friends and I help each other out, and we don't really hide anything from each other. And when we connect on something, watch out! When we all have the same mindset, we can do some amazing things.

When we are together, we don't just hang out and act silly, though. We also talk about anything and everything. Whether it's what happened to us that day or week, something we did or the never-boring topic of girls, we say what we feel.

> **If you don't have your friends, who do you have?**

We support each other when needed by lending a hand, helping cheer each other up and even giving that almighty dollar.

We've had times when we needed to be strong and help each other out, and the strength of our friendship was really tested.

5. **Show of Friendship**

I received the support I needed from my friends when my brother, Fred, left home. Fred is three years older than me (I'm 17) and we share a close relationship, so when he left home, I had a lot of angry feelings inside.

We used to do all kinds of things together, so when he first left,

I felt as if I'd lost an arm or something. But my friends saw how I was feeling and kept my spirits up. Leon came by the house to see me, Eric would hang with me at the church and Ivan showed up all the time.

This helped me forget about what had happened and think about what I still had: good friends and family. The way they reached out to me really showed me how strong our friendship was.

6. Help from the Leader

I didn't get to know Leon that well until last year because he was really Fred's friend. We mostly kept our distance with a "Hi-Bye" relationship.

But when my brother left, Leon started coming by the house to talk to my parents and hang with me. He helped me deal with Fred leaving by just listening to what I had to say and sometimes by telling me what I should do. I think Leon missed Fred a little too, but we learned to move on.

> **I received the support I needed from my friends when my brother, Fred, left home.**

My friends and I also had to come together when Leon had a crisis: he went into the hospital because he was depressed. When I went to visit him, I felt really bad because I saw how Leon was changing and I couldn't do anything about it. He wasn't talking much, and he just acted…different.

There was tension among all of us because nobody really knew what to say at first. It was hard to joke around with him in the beginning, but the tension died down with each visit.

Every visit we made to the hospital, we talked, laughed, and we prayed with Leon. He looked stronger each time we came back. When he came out, he looked like the good old Leon that we knew.

7. **Thinking About Friendship and the Future**

That incident helped us draw closer to Leon because the way he started to improve showed us that having support from his friends had an impact.

The way we helped each other through hard times showed me (and probably all of us) how much our friendship means to us.

In the future, I hope we can keep our friendship intact. We talk about our plans for the future all the time. Whatever we end up doing, we hope to link up later on in life (share an apartment or visit each other) and to make something positive out of our lives. I think the similar values we share will help us stay strong as friends.

It seems like almost everyone is looking for this kind of acceptance, but teenagers often seem to look to a popular clique or a gang or similar organization to get that group feeling.

Most of these groups force you to do something wrong or something you may not like in order to join. They try to turn you into something you are not. That's not the way it is with us.

What I like best about my friends is that they let me be myself, and support me for who I am.

The Crew
from the Parking Lot

By Ferentz Lafargue

1.   The parking lot behind Wertheimer's department store on Jamaica Avenue was once a place where a lot of boyhood dreams were born. Dreams of growing up and playing for the Yankees or Giants someday, dreams of meeting that girl, the one you knew was out there, the one that was made for you. My friends and I used to spend the whole afternoon there playing baseball, football, manhunt, and practically anything else you could think of.

One day we noticed a piece of wood in the corner of the lot. We found a rock to prop it up and made ourselves a bicycle ramp. We practiced jumping for a week or two until the wood broke and it was back to playing bike tag and waiting for the next thing to come along.

Every winter when it snowed, there would be huge piles of snow in the corners of the lot. We would start out by doing some light skiing to get warmed up and soften up the snow. (The skis were made of the finest cardboard we could find.) But we all know what happens when you put a bunch of guys somewhere with snow...SNOWFIGHT!!

The rules were simple: whichever mountain you were on was your territory and whoever was with you was your team. We would fight until one team captured the other team's mountain or the teams split up and everyone started fighting amongst themselves. When that happened it was every man for himself. We would go home looking like we had just climbed Mt. Everest and

---

(All names have been changed.)

sometimes I think that would have been easier.

2. We Were a Team

We also shared a lot of disappointments in the parking lot. We felt bad for Ed when he didn't make the varsity basketball team. We felt sorry when Devon's girl Wendy moved away. (They were the royal couple of the parking lot.) When Abner and Carlos were sent to fight in the Persian Gulf War we all kept an eye on the news. There weren't any me's or I's in the parking lot—we were a team.

But these days the parking lot is just used for parking cars. We don't even keep in touch like we used to. Rarely will you see two of us together. Some have moved away, the rest just feel like they're miles away. At least to me they do. The only thing we all have in common is that we grew up.

When I look around now and see people that I used to be down with back in the days, I feel really sorry for some of these guys.

Devon was the superstar of the parking lot. He could throw, run, catch—the whole nine. We used to think he was the total package. We thought he would play high school baseball or football, then get drafted or get a scholarship, and go on to become a major leaguer. But instead of going out for one of the teams, he opted to be down with the fellas, hanging out and doing things like robbing people, stealing chains or getting caught up in stupid gang battles.

3. Rikers, Here I Come

Now he's one of the people who comes up to me and talks about how he messed up, how he should have stayed in school. Now the only things he strives for are his own apartment, a G.E.D., a job and a car. Devon's only 18 and has been sent to Rikers Island jail two times already. The sad thing is he has no fear of going back.

Devon's younger brother John was a pretty good ballplayer too but more importantly he was a B+ student and a born leader.

He was never afraid of being team captain. In fact, he thrived on it. He used to talk about joining the Marines and getting his M-14. Now John is 17 and has a kid and he's not even close to a high school diploma. He was hardly ever in school last year. The word is that John is dealing guns. An M-14 is probably child's play compared to some of the guns he's come in contact with.

Then there's Angel. Angel used to be my best friend and in a way he always will be. Angel had drive and determination. One summer he lost his glove and, being that he was the only lefty in the parking lot, he had no one to lend him one. But Angel decided not to let that keep him on the sidelines. He found a right-handed glove and for about a year and a half he tried to be right-handed. He started doing almost everything right-handed.

> **When I look around now and see people that I used to be down with back in the days, I feel really sorry for some of these guys.**

Eventually he got another left-handed glove. But even after that you could occasionally see him tricking an opposing batter with a wicked right-handed curve ball. Angel hasn't dropped out yet, not officially, but I doubt he goes to school more than five full days a year. When he does go he usually cuts out early in the day. Now Angel's dealing drugs. He used to have determination but these days the only thing he seems determined to do is mess up his life.

4. Role Model?

The sad thing is that these are the guys that little kids look up to. The other day me and one of my friends were walking down 89th Avenue and one of my little brother's friends came up to us with a fake blunt that he had rolled up, and was telling us how good it was. This kid is 10 years old at most. But you really can't blame him. That's what he sees around him. That's what's considered cool.

The ones that plan to go on to college—as soon as they're finished and have some money in the bank, they move as far away from the neighborhood as fast as they can. My homeboy Abner, for example, hasn't even graduated from college yet and he's already beginning the process. He recently moved to Forest Hills and if it weren't for his parents you'd never see his face around the block at all.

He even started to forget people's names. There's one girl he's known for about 10 or 15 years now and the other day he couldn't come up with her name. It made me wonder if he remembers mine.

5. **I'm Their Last, Best Hope**

Then there's me. I was the youngest kid in the parking lot, which meant I was last to get picked for the teams and the first to get picked on. I was like everyone's little brother. I never made it to the forefront; I just stood back and watched everyone else. I looked up to these guys. But I knew the real them. I was smart enough to learn from their mistakes.

They still keep an eye out for me. Every time one of them sees one of my articles or hears about me doing anything else good, he's always ready to congratulate me and tell me to keep it up. It's almost like I'm their last hope of success: if I come out OK then they'll honestly be able to say they had a hand in raising me.

I intend to go to college and study communications and advertising. Hopefully one day I'll be writing for a big-time newspaper, or working for an advertising company. Then I'd like to make sure my little brother gets his act together, help fix up my neighborhood, and do whatever I can to help out some of my old friends. But whatever I end up doing, one thing I won't do is let those guys down and mess up my life.

Writing this article I discovered I'm a pretty lucky guy after all. Remembering all those good times we had in the parking lot was enough to make me cry. I hope everyone has a parking lot in their lives. What good is a tree without roots?

Girl, Stop Fronting! I Reached Out to My Archenemy

By Chantel Clark

1.   Throughout high school, I had such resentment for Kim. She was dark-skinned with short hair she often wore in braided extensions. Every month she mixed in a different color—blue, red, neon pink. She had boyish features but the body of a woman. And she was loud for no damn reason. I think she just liked to hear herself talk.

Kim was quick to curse someone out who she felt needed to get checked. She'd get nasty with you in a heartbeat! She was rude, but intelligent, a secret I figured out when I had math with her and was amazed that this "ghetto fabulous" girl was so smart.

She was also a comedian. I must admit she could make me laugh. She seemed to have a carefree attitude, not caring what people thought or said, dressing how she wanted regardless of trends.

Me, I was in my glory. I was a trendsetter, following my own dress code, just not to the same extremes. I looked like I was going somewhere exclusive every time I came to school. My friends joked that I was going to the clubs every day because I wore makeup and dressed up 95% of the time.

Plus, I was in hair school on the side, so you know a sister was sporting every hairstyle in creation. I was a real vain person on the outside, but inside I was constantly trying to understand who I was.

2. **Fighting Over He-Said, She-Said**

Kim and I had different styles, but we were a lot alike, and we found each other threatening because of that. In freshman year, we got into a fight. She started it over some he-said, she-said. I wanted to avoid it, but people were all around and I couldn't chump up.

I won and gained my respect. After that, I had to live up to my reputation of being all that and a bag of chips. So when I walked past her, I had nothing to say. And classmates added to our rivalry, saying things like, "That's why Chantel won," or "Chantel got up in her face."

After that, Kim and I constantly bumped heads. If we saw each other in the mall, we'd roll our eyes at each other. If we saw each other at a party, we made it our business to walk past each other with disgust.

But when I came back to school senior year after summer vacation, I saw my arch-enemy and she was no longer the same. She seemed to have fallen apart. She didn't do her hair or dress nice anymore. She didn't even hang out with her group of friends.

> **Throughout high school, I had such resentment for Kim.**

Normally, this would be bait, a perfect opportunity to make her feel down and out. Sure enough, I began to see people picking on her for no reason, calling her names, throwing things at her and starting fights.

3. **I Wanted to Reach Out**

Her face wore more pain than a woman in labor; her eyes held a sadness that was undefined. I heard through people that Kim was homeless. In fact, I heard her mom kicked her out for a man, and forced her to live in a shed in the backyard. I heard she barely ate, and she was getting skinny. Her face looked like death, and honestly, I was worried.

For the first time, I actually didn't want to pick an argument with her. I knew the pain she wore—that face was a face I had hidden inside. And now it was staring back at me like a reflection in my mirror.

I know pain firsthand, and it's weird—once you've been hurt or gone through some trials, it's like you know when someone else is hurting inside. You can sense it, you can feel it. I had a yearning inside to talk to her, because I was sure I could speak to her like no one else could.

> **Kim and I had different styles, but we were a lot alike, and we found each other threatening because of that.**

You see, my mom chose men over me, so I know the feeling. And my aunt did the same thing to my cousin. I come from a family of broken women and misleading men, so I understood her pain.

4. My Pride Kept Me Still

One day, I went to a social worker in my school, Ms. Bee, who many girls talked to. In her office, I saw Kim crying. I felt a heaviness on my chest. I wanted to reach out to her, but I couldn't.

God forbid I try to talk to her. What would people think? I also thought to myself, "What if I'm trying to be nice and this chick gets smart? I might curse her out." So my pride, my temper and my attitude kept me still.

I left Ms. Bee's office wondering what I could do. How could I speak to her? What would she say?

I returned to Ms. Bee's office later that day and asked her what was wrong with Kim, but she knew of our rivalry and said it was confidential. So I asked Ms. Bee if she could set up a meeting between me and Kim. I explained that I saw how much pain she was in and wanted to help in any way I could.

Ms. Bee was shocked, but she knew my life story and that I'd be able to say things that only the two of us could understand.

5. **Strong Enough to Overcome**

About a week or so later, Ms. Bee called me into her office, and Kim was there. I suddenly felt out of place, but I came in anyway.

I said to her, "I came from a broken home. My life was never a bowl of cherries. My mother, a drug abuser. My father, missing in action. No one knew when he would pop up. My family has more stories than an old Negro testimonial, but I was strong enough to overcome." I told her, "You're beautiful and strong, and if you ever need a shoulder to cry on, I'm here."

She was shocked, looking at me with this face that said, "No way." I guess she never saw me as the type to have a hard life, because I hide it so well. So I had to say, "Yes, it's true."

6. **No Fairy Princess in a Castle**

After that, we heard each other's stories. We quickly became friends because we shared similar lives, building a friendship out of past hurt and pain.

Kim told me about her mom, and how it felt to be forced to live in a shed. She said that her mom took away all her clothes that she'd worked hard to buy and gave them to her sisters. So now she was stealing to survive.

I told her about my drug-abusing mother and my good-for-nothing father. How at 5 I almost died because my uncle got high and started a fire. I told her that my dad slept with my aunt, my aunt's daughter, and eventually tried to sleep with me.

I told her how this fairy princess in a glass castle is my image, but it's only a lie. We told each other things that almost nobody knew, and we laughed about it, too. It's crazy, but I do find my life funny—how could you not? And laughing about it helps me get through it.

After that conversation, we trusted each other. People often stared at us and talked behind our backs, because we were once enemies, now friends. They couldn't understand the relationship we had.

Kim needed me as her support system, her friend. I made it my duty to give her what she needed. I gave her clothes, lent her money, snuck her in my house to eat and to hang out. We became like sisters.

7. Becoming True Friends

I helped her to find herself again. And in return, I found me. By showing who we really were, we realized we could both change, be ourselves. She recognized that those pink braids were for getting attention. She didn't need to be loud and vulgar to be respected. That was just a front. So she changed.

She also stopped blaming herself for the way her mother treated her and for the way she had to live. We talked a lot about living life to the fullest, despite the cards God dealt us. And she began to feel determined to survive what her mom was putting her through. Eventually Kim started acting like parts of her old self again, the girl who I could talk bull to, and she would come right back with a remark.

Kim gave me emotional support as well, even about little things. I found out I didn't need to wear a lot of makeup to be me. I was just as pretty without it. More than that, though, I found out that I didn't have to pretend all the time, that I could be me without worrying about what anyone else thinks.

Kim and I realized we could be honest with each other. We both needed one real person in our lives—someone who didn't care if your feelings got hurt or you got mad, as long as she told you the truth.

My Boy Had a Boyfriend

By Odé A. Manderson

1.   Once, I overheard a conversation between two older guys. One of them said he had a friend who was gay. The dude responded by saying:

"I oughta kick your butt for telling me that. Get your gay butt outta here."

Even though I'm straight, it makes my stomach turn to hear comments like that.

2. **But I Use the 'F' Word**

Still I admit that I have used the word "f-g" when I've wanted to insult someone. It's hypocritical and I'm trying to stop using the term, but old habits die hard sometimes.

And even though I don't consider myself to be homophobic (prejudiced against gays), I used to think that gays act outrageously because of how they're portrayed on TV and film. Since I usually didn't run into anybody who acted in that way, I thought gays lived in a separate world.

But I've been in contact with gays and didn't know it. My college advisor mentioned that he was gay during an assembly. I didn't think too much about it, though. I still didn't think that I would ever meet someone like me, but gay.

Then, during my job as a Summer Youth Employment Program (SYEP) employee two years ago, I met Thomas.

(All names have been changed.)

73

3. **We Were Cool**

On my first day of work, he introduced himself to me, and quickly became a good friend.

He was cool. I learned a lot from him, like how to take initiative when times called for it and to speak my mind. He had a sense of humor, and he was straightforward about everything.

> I didn't think that I would ever meet someone like me, but gay.

We eventually started to hang out on the weekends. Sometimes we chilled at a mall. Other times we would hang out at a diner on the corner after picking up our paychecks. Or we would go to his cousin's crib, where we watched cable or listened to music.

When we were hanging out, I sometimes thought Thomas might be gay. But I didn't want to jump to conclusions, so I never said anything about it. You can't tell someone's sexuality that easily. I didn't want to label Thomas as gay unless I heard it come straight from his mouth. We were cool, so it didn't matter.

4. **He Began to Back Off**

But toward the end of July, Thomas started going from being outspoken to quiet, and I wondered what was going on. I came home from work one day, and the phone rang. It was him.

"What the hell is the matter with you n-gga? Dyin' or something?" I demanded.

He started to say something smart, but stopped. He put down the receiver. A few seconds later, someone picked it up.

"Hello?"

It was one of his cousins.

"Look," she started. "Thomas has something to say to you, but he's too shy to say it. Do you know what it is?"

I wasn't a total idiot. Or so I thought.

"Does it have anything to do with his sexual orientation?" I asked.

"Yes it does. That's not all though. The reason why he had a hard time telling you was because he has a crush on you."

5. **Dealing With the Shock**

I was shocked. Butterflies fluttered in my gut, then turned into angry hornets. Then a bright-colored spot appeared in front of my eyes. I was silent for a moment before I decided to say something. I was prepared to hear him tell me he was gay, not that he had it for me.

His cousin said that he liked me because of my looks and personality. I blinked hard.

"Tell him he has nothing to be shy about," I replied, trying to compose myself. "Put him on the phone."

I heard a faint "here" as she passed the receiver to Thomas.

"Yeah."

"That's all you had to tell me? Look, it was none of my business, so trusting me...that was strong of you. And it won't change anything, if that's what you're thinking. I'm cool."

6. **We Still Hung Out**

After that, we still hung out, even though we didn't talk about his sexual orientation or his crush. I didn't want to bring anything up. I was thinking of how I would take it if I were gay and a straight friend started asking me about it. I thought that would make me feel uncomfortable and that I might say something stupid that would make him feel uncomfortable.

I wanted to know if he was happy with himself, even if people didn't accept him. But I didn't ask. I didn't want to make him feel like he was on trial for being who he was. I also wondered if he still had a crush on me. When girls liked me, I felt a sense of satisfaction. But with Thomas, I felt bewildered. The idea of any guy liking me caught me off guard.

7. A Harsh Response

Right after I hung up the phone with Thomas I had called my good friend Darnell because I needed some feedback. The minute I explained what happened, he burst out laughing.

"Odé, that's the worst," he said in between snickers.

"He's in love with you, baaaaaabeeeeeeeeee…" he added in a sing-song voice. "I would've screamed on him," he suddenly stated coldly.

"For what?" I said. "He knows where I stand, so it's not a problem. Plus, he's peoples."

"True, true," Darnell said. "I still would've screamed on him," he said.

But I didn't want Thomas to feel bad that he'd told me. He probably thought I wouldn't take it in a civilized manner. After hearing how kids our age treat gays—the threats, the jokes and the violence—he was probably scared that I'd go and wild out.

8. Straight People Spread Rumors

The minute a straight person thinks something is up, they're likely to tell their friends and it'll start a big thing. Your rep may never be the same.

For instance, at my job, many employees caught on to Thomas's feminine mannerisms.

"Is he gay?" female counselors would ask me.

"Yo, is that n-gga gay or somethin'?" the male counselors would ask accusatorily, as if it was my fault. Then they'd add, "Yeah, he's gay."

Because of attitudes like that, I think that gay teens are forced to live life differently than straight teens. They have to be careful what they say and do in front of other people. Most people only want to know if someone is gay so they can go in for the attack.

9. We Talked About His Relationships

So I tried to be very respectful of Thomas, even though I

wasn't perfect. And Thomas would sometimes bring up stuff on his sexuality. Those talks let me know where he was coming from.

One time we started discussing relationships, and we swapped stories. His boyfriends were usually four to five years older than him, and he had been in a couple long-term relationships.

He would talk about how guys treated him and how he felt about the person he was dating, but he didn't go into detail. I didn't ask for more information because I didn't want to overstep my boundaries as a friend.

For the rest of August, we hung out as much as we used to before Thomas came out. The only time I felt uncomfortable was when I let my tongue slip sometimes, saying "f-g" near him. I'd want to kick myself because I didn't know how Thomas took it. It didn't seem

> **The idea of any guy liking me caught me off guard.**

to bother him, and that really threw me off. It made me feel stupid, because I felt disrespectful.

After a little while, I stopped wondering if he still had a crush on me. It didn't matter. Even if he still had feelings for me, it wasn't changing our friendship.

10. What if My Own Son...

But when the summer ended, we didn't keep in touch. I began lifeguard training and went back to school. He was trying to get another job. We weren't able to chill as much because we had less time.

He called a couple of times just to see how I was holding up and what I had been doing, but he didn't ask to hang out. Neither did I. I figured he just didn't want to hang out anymore. I don't know why.

Even though we're not friends anymore, I'm glad that Thomas had the guts to come out. I'm impressed that he kept it real and revealed who he was.

And I think our friendship showed me how my perceptions of gay people were pretty off. In reality, signs of gayness are nowhere near as cut and dried as they seem on TV.

Thomas made me realize that gay people aren't so stereotypical, and have things in common with straight people. Thomas had some of the stereotypes in the way he walked and talked, but he was also reserved and thoughtful.

I've realized I don't live in a separate world from gay people and I don't want to discriminate against them. Ten years from now a gay person could be my boss or my son's godfather. For all I know, my son could be gay. And I wouldn't love him any less.

The Bully

By Paul Langan

With a cold November wind stabbing through his jacket, Darrell Mercer took one last walk with his best friend, Malik Stone.

"Man, I can't believe you're movin' to California tomorrow," Malik said. "I just can't believe I won't see you no more."

Darrell shook his head. He could not believe it either. In just a few hours, he would leave the only neighborhood he had ever known in his fifteen years. Soon his street, his school, and every friend he had in the world would be thousands of miles away. Thinking about what was ahead of him, Darrell felt like a man going to his own hanging.

"I'll miss you, man," Darrell said, his voice wavering.

The boys had known each other since first grade at Harrison School on 44th Street. Their neighborhood was definitely not one of Philadelphia's best. Most of the buildings were old and decaying, and graffiti covered just about every one. Some houses were vacant, and a few had broken windows. Abandoned cars rusted along many streets, and occasionally local newscasts would run a story about city crime and feature this area as an example. To many people, the neighborhood was trouble, but to Darrell and his friends, it was home. True, there were guys selling drugs on street corners. But there were also good kids like Malik, Big Reggie, and Mark. Because of them, Darrell had never felt alone.

Inside the rundown homes that lined Darrell's block, there

This is Chapter 1 from The Bully by Paul Langan in the Bluford Series. Copyright 2002 © by Townsend Press. Reprinted with permission. www.townsendpress.com

were always people to turn to in times of trouble. Across the street was old Mr. Corbitt, who sat on his porch each day and waved at everyone who passed by. And in the corner house was Mrs. Morton. She made sweet-potato pie for people in the neighborhood, especially Darrell and his mother.

"This'll help you grow," Mrs. Morton would say whenever she left a pie at their apartment. It never seemed to work, but Darrell didn't mind because the pies were delicious.

Darrell had always been short for his age. At fifteen years old, he was just under five feet. He was also skinny, without a respectable muscle in his small body. Back in September, Darrell had dreaded starting Franklin High, but his friends were right there with him. If anyone picked on Darrell during those first weeks of school, they had the other guys to deal with too. But all that was changing.

Darrell was moving to California two months after the school year had begun. It was the first day of high school all over again, only this time Darrell did not have his friends to protect him. Darrell did not admit it to anyone, but he was scared.

"Want a cheesesteak?" Malik asked when they came to Sal's Steaks.

"I guess," Darrell said. Sal made the best cheesesteaks in the neighborhood, or maybe in the entire city. They were loaded with gobs of dripping cheese and just the right amount of fried onions.

"This one's on me," Malik said, a crack in his voice. Physically, Malik was the opposite of Darrell. He was six feet tall with big muscular shoulders. Although he was just a freshman, Malik had already earned a position on the Franklin High School varsity football team. Ever since they were young boys, Darrell was thankful that he was Malik's friend because nobody messed with Malik or his friends. Watching Malik return with the steaks, Darrell felt a wave of sadness sweep over him.

"This is our last cheesesteak together," Malik said, handing one to Darrell.

"Thanks, Malik," Darrell said. Normally, he would devour the cheesesteak quickly, but now, for the first time he could remember, he felt as if he could not eat. His throat seemed to close up on him. *It isn't fair*, he thought. Why did things happen this way? Why did he have to leave his home and his best friends? And why, of all times, did it have to be in the middle of his first year of high school? He knew why. His mother had explained it many times, but she could not change how he felt. Realizing he would hurt Malik's feelings if he did not accept his gift, Darrell forced the cheesesteak down his throat. He knew it would be the last meal he would ever have with his friend.

The boys continued walking down the darkening street. Every storefront was painful for Darrell to see. He knew he would not be back to the old neighborhood again, at least not for a long time. He glanced across the street at the old grocery store. Today it looked warm and inviting, even though the owners charged too much for meats, and the fruits and vegetables were not always fresh. At the corner, they passed the Laundromat where his mother did her wash. A black mechanical rocking horse stood next to the door so parents could entertain their children while waiting for the laundry to dry. Once, Darrell and Malik gave coins to a little neighborhood kid so he could ride.

"Remember when Rasheed took four rides on our money?" Darrell asked.

"Yeah," Malik said glumly.

It was dark now. Mom had asked Darrell to be home early. The bus was leaving at 5:15 the next morning.

Darrell looked down at the emerald-green shards of a shattered beer bottle glistening in the street light. "I guess I gotta go now, Malik," he said heavily. "I gotta go home."

Home. What a mockery that word was now, Darrell thought. Home was an empty apartment with boxes in the middle of the floor, packed for the move to California. Mrs. Morton was handling the shipping for them.

"You been a real brother to me," Darrell said. "I...I love you, man," Darrell blurted, his voice melting into embarrassing sobs.

Malik grabbed Darrell and gave him a bear hug. For a second, Darrell's face was jammed into Malik's shirt. Then the two separated, and, without a word, started walking in opposite directions. After a few steps, Darrell began to run.

"It's not fair!" he yelled, as he sprinted through the dark. He felt as if he were being robbed, that things were being taken from him that he could never replace.

Sure, Malik would miss him, Darrell thought, but Malik was big, and he had tons of friends. Darrell was sure Malik would be fine without him.

But Darrell was not so certain about his own future. The days ahead stretched out before him like a dark road filled with dangerous shadows. It would be like the summer Mom sent him to a camp for inner-city kids. The camp director promised Darrell and his mother that he would experience adventures in the outdoors away from the dangers of the city. What Darrell ended up experiencing was torment from a kid who wanted nothing more than to make anyone weaker than him feel as miserable as possible.

The kid's name was Jermaine, and his favorite activity was torturing Darrell. He pushed Darrell into the lake. He dropped worms into Darrell's ice cream. He put laxative in Darrell's pudding, making him sick for two days. During the whole time at camp, Darrell remained silent about Jermaine. What choice did he have? He knew he did not stand a chance against Jermaine in a fight, and he knew if he told one of the adults, Jermaine would retaliate the next time no one was watching. But the biggest reason Darrell never said anything to anyone was that he was ashamed of being so helpless. At least if he kept everything to himself, no one else would know how pathetic he was. Lately, whenever Darrell thought about California, he imagined some kid like Jermaine waiting for him. Or maybe several Jermaines. And nobody would be there to help him. Not Malik. Not anyone.

As Darrell walked down the alley towards his apartment, a stray cat greeted him. It purred and rubbed its face against his calf, looking up at him with radiant green eyes.

"This is it, Max," Darrell said, petting the cat's soft gray fur. "Your last pet from me. Goodbye, Max." The cat circled his legs.

Darrell and his mother had lived in the apartment for six years. Before that, they lived in a small house. Darrell's father was with them then, but he was killed in a car accident. After his death, Darrell's mother got a job as a clerk for an insurance agency, and they moved to the apartment.

For years, everything had been fine, but then in August a larger insurance company bought out the agency where Darrell's mother worked. To save money, the company eliminated her job along with hundreds of others. For a while, she tried to find work nearby that would pay her enough to support the two of them, but the only jobs she could find were in fast-food restaurants. Then in October, Darrell's Uncle Jason, her brother, called and offered her a job in California paying twice what she could make in their neighborhood. Darrell understood why his mother chose to take the job, but he did not like her decision. *I wish he never would have called*, Darrell thought as he walked up the steps to the apartment.

"Hi, baby," his mother said as she opened the door.

Darrell tried to hurry to his room and shield his face from his mother. He did not want her to notice he had been crying.

"Are you okay?" she asked, reaching an arm out to comfort him.

"I'm fine," Darrell said, wishing she would leave him alone. He felt bad enough without his mom fussing over him.

"Oh, baby, I know how hard it is for you to leave your friends, especially in the middle of the school year. It hurts me so much to be doing this to you. If there was any other way..."

"It's okay," Darrell replied.

"You know if I hadn't gotten laid off—"

"Mom, I'm telling you, it's okay," Darrell insisted.

"Your Uncle Jason promising me that job in California seemed like a godsend. I got no choice," she said, putting her hand on his shoulder.

He had heard it all before, and he knew it was true. It only made Darrell angrier knowing his mother was right. If she were doing this for some selfish reason, then he could be mad at her, and it would almost feel better. "Mom, stop callin' me 'baby,' okay?"

Darrell escaped to his bedroom and sat on the bed he would use one more night. His suitcase sat alone in the middle of the floor, ready for the morning. The room where he once felt so comfortable, his cave, was no more. All his posters had been stripped from the walls.

Sitting in the dark room by himself, Darrell wanted to do something crazy, anything to avoid moving away from home. *Maybe I could run away tonight and hide in one of those empty warehouses on 35th Street*, he thought. But then he remembered his mother. There was no way he would put her through that. Instead, he stretched out on his bed and stared at the ceiling, waiting for the day to arrive.

In the morning, just before sunrise, Darrell and his mother grabbed their two suitcases and climbed aboard the westward-bound bus. Darrell stared out the window as his neighborhood passed by him for the last time. His mother talked nonstop in a nervous monologue. Darrell paid little attention.

"Darrell, just give it a chance. You might like California. Uncle Jason said our new neighborhood is much nicer than here. He said the houses are well kept, and we'll be close to the stadium, and you can see baseball and football games."

Darrell closed his eyes and resolved to hate California no matter what anybody said.

"Jason also said the school you'll be going to is pretty new. It's an old neighborhood, but the school is only about fifteen years old. It's called Bluford High. It's named for an African American astronaut," his mother went on.

Darrell closed his eyes and said nothing. He knew his silence would hurt his mother's feelings. But he could not help it. Nothing she could say would convince him that he'd like California.

"Oh, honey," she added, "if you'd just give it a chance."

Darrell sank deeper into his seat.

"I hated to leave my friends too, Darrell," she continued. "I made some wonderful friends at the office and on our street, and I won't know anybody in California either except for my brother and his family."

It's different with you, Mom, Darrell thought. *You make friends easily. I'll be in class with kids who've gone through middle school together and had two months in high school to get used to each other. They'll see this kid from Philadelphia who looks twelve years old, and I'm in for it.* Yet he said nothing. He did not feel like explaining things to his mother. She would only worry about him even more.

"Just put a big, friendly smile on your face your first day there, honey, and by the end of the day you'll have at least one nice friend," she said.

Maybe that worked in first grade when everybody was wearing name tags and kids hadn't learned to be mean to each other yet, Darrell thought. But kids learn fast. By third grade, Darrell was glad he had Malik, Big Reggie, and Mark.

But now, he wouldn't have anybody.

Everything Darrell knew and loved was gone. And though she meant well, his mother had no idea how hard it was to be the new kid in school, especially one who is smaller than everyone else.

Darrell remembered that his Uncle Jason was well over six feet tall. A few years ago, he came to Philadelphia to visit, and he looked at then twelve-year old Darrell and said in a booming voice, "Will you look at that boy? Why is he so skinny? Nobody in our family was ever that small at his age! Jackie, ain't you feedin' him enough?"

His mother seemed defensive. "Oh, he'll hit his growth spurt anytime now," she said, "He'll shoot up like a spring weed. Then you won't even recognize him, Jason."

Remembering that conversation, Darrell could only think one thing—his mother was wrong.

She refused to accept the truth, Darrell thought. And the truth was that he was still a short, underweight kid, and all the hopes and smiles in the world were not going to change that.

Darrell gazed out the window while the bus raced farther and farther from his home. A feeling of dread weighed heavily on him as the sun crawled slowly into the sky.

You can read the rest of this story in The Bully, *by Paul Langan.*

THE REAL WORLD
Meet the People in My World

A Sad Silence: Aunt Sheila Had AIDS

By Desirée Guéry

1. There was a secret in my family that went on for years. Well, it wasn't a secret to everyone, only to me. One day, on a drive home with my dad, he told me, "Your Aunt Sheila is sick."

Aunt Sheila was my father's sister, my Titi. We were close and spoke on the phone about every two weeks. I thought it was strange that she didn't tell me herself that she was sick.

"Sick?" I asked curiously. "With the flu?"

"No, she has AIDS," he said blankly, staring at the scenery outside. He said it as if it were no big deal, as if it wouldn't affect me.

2. **I Had No Idea What AIDS Was**

Being only 8 or 9, I didn't understand what AIDS is. I had no idea it's a deadly disease. I just nodded, thinking nothing of it. My father didn't make a big deal of it, and they were close, so I figured it wasn't a big deal. I had no idea how devastated I'd feel later on.

My mother, who I was closer to, talked to me more about it later that night. Titi Sheila had wanted to keep her illness a secret from me so that she could find a way to tell me herself.

Mom said she caught the disease from someone she loved and trusted—her fiancé. I didn't understand what she meant when she said Titi got the disease from her partner, but I didn't ask any questions since Mom said I wasn't supposed to know. I thought maybe Mom didn't want to tell me much so that the news would still be somewhat fresh when Titi told me. But Titi didn't bring it up.

> **There was a secret in my family that went on for years.**

I saw her a few times after my talk with my parents during her yearly visits from Montreal, Canada, where she lived. She looked as I always remembered her: healthy. She had meat on her bones and looked vivacious and gorgeous in clothes she made herself. (She was a fashion designer.)

I always looked forward to her visits and our shopping trips in the Village, where she'd buy scarves and purses. She was free-spirited, fun, fashionable and loving.

3. **Learned More at School**

I didn't know how to bring up Titi's illness when I was with her, so I didn't. But I began to better understand what she had when I learned about AIDS in the 6th and 7th grades.

I soon realized that AIDS was a condition that developed from being infected with HIV, a virus you get through unprotected sex or the sharing of needles. Because of the AIDS virus, her immune system had shut down.

Because her immune system wasn't working, it was harder for her to fight off other viruses, such as a cold or the flu. Catching those viruses could lead to bigger illnesses as well.

My classmates seemed like they couldn't care less about the topic, but it was frightening for me to learn about a disease that hit so close to home.

I couldn't keep my emotions bottled up. I often cried in class. One of my best friends at the time, Jackie, would console me. I'd told her about Titi Sheila's condition. I trusted her and it was comforting to have a shoulder to cry on and a friend to talk to who knew just as much about the disease as I did.

4. I Wanted to Know How She Felt

Still, I felt horrible about never hearing the words come straight from Titi Sheila's mouth about her condition. I think I would've understood her illness more if we'd discussed it. I wanted her to tell me how she felt. I hate not knowing how she felt then, and I hate knowing that she'll never be able to tell me.

She probably wasn't comfortable discussing it with me, even though when we talked, I told her whatever was on my mind. I wish she'd done the same. At times, I felt like she didn't trust me, or thought I couldn't handle her condition.

Maybe I never gave her the opportunity to talk to me about her illness since I was often so busy talking about a celebrity crush I had or something that happened in school. But I figured that if she didn't want to tell me about her illness, I shouldn't ask.

5. Stick Thin...

But the changes I soon noticed spoke mountains. When I was 13, Titi Sheila visited us. Her physical appearance had changed dramatically. Her personality was still lively and bubbly, but she was stick thin.

I'd never seen her that thin before. I was scared for her; I knew she must be really sick. I remember her showing my mother and me how she had to wear extra clothes and "butt pads" under her jeans to make them fit.

Even with all the extra layers and padding, she was the thinnest person I'd ever seen. I overheard her telling my mother she'd lost her appetite.

"I can barely keep anything down," she said. I understood much more about the disease at this point, but didn't know that AIDS could cause you to lose your appetite and weight.

6. **...And Sickly**

She was always catching small colds, the sniffles, stomachaches and headaches. Even though these are normal things people catch, for Titi, it was bad. Her immune system was shut down, so a simple cold could turn into pneumonia. Titi often had to go to the hospital.

> I didn't know how to bring up Titi's illness when I was with her, so I didn't.

Titi Sheila still wouldn't tell me about her illness, even though she must've known I could see how poor her health was. Three years ago, in August, she was on vacation and got sick. "I was at the hotel for most of the trip," she told me when she got home. "I just kept throwing up. It's just a small stomach bug. It'll go away." It didn't. She was admitted to the hospital a week after arriving home.

My parents and I visited her in the hospital in Montreal that December. To see her so sick, barely able to do anything herself, not even able to stay awake, hurt me more than any physical pain I'd experienced. I cried all day, and it was hard, because I didn't want her to see me cry.

I knew it might be the last time I'd ever see her since she was so sick. I couldn't handle the thought of growing up without her humor, love, guidance, understanding and support.

I wanted so badly to tell her that I knew, since I knew I'd

probably never have the chance to talk to her about it again. But I just couldn't. I didn't know how to say it, or how she'd react, so I brought up other things.

7. Phone Call at 2 A.M.

A few weeks after we got back home, my grandmother, who was still with Titi at the hospital, said that Titi was feeling better. We were relieved.

Then, two weeks later (the day before I was scheduled to take an important test) the phone rang at 2 in the morning.

After Mom got off the phone, she started crying. She turned to me and said, "Sheila didn't make it." We both cried on the couch, and I cried myself to sleep that night. I couldn't believe she'd passed so suddenly when we thought she was getting better.

I didn't go to her funeral, which was held in Canada. I wanted to remember Titi for what she'd given to me and shown me throughout the years, and that's how I remember her now.

8. Wanted to Be by Myself

Still, I felt awful. Mom was concerned. "Do you want to talk to me about it?" she asked. "How do you feel?" I just avoided her questions by telling her I wanted to be alone or had nothing to say. She wanted to be there for me, but I wanted to be by myself. Maybe that's how Titi Sheila felt when she was sick.

I never talked to anyone about my feelings over her death, even though it's affected me deeply. I wonder how dealing with Titi's illness would've been different if we'd talked about it. I think we would've become even closer. But I'll never know, and maybe that's just how she wanted it.

My Father: Guilty or Innocent?

By T. Shawn Welcome

1.   My father was very popular in Guyana, South America, where we lived until I was 9 years old. I could only wonder why he was so popular because I never spent time with my father. I only saw him on those rare occasions when he slept at home.

But despite his faults, I still admired my father. When his friends heard me speak they'd say, "That's Terry's son alright." I was just like my dad, and I felt proud to be like him. He was my role model.

After we moved to America he and my mother started to fight constantly. I hated when they fought, because he'd hit her. He started disappearing for days and then weeks at a time. I'd only see him on weekends. One weekend, he took my brother and me to a Yankee game. I don't like baseball; the only thing I liked about the game was that he was there.

2. Weekends

But the thing I remember the most was the weekend when he taught my brother Rob and me how to ride bicycles at the track and field next to Yankee Stadium. I remember going down the straightaway part of the track with my pops at my side. I felt a bond with him.

Those weekends were great but they didn't last. When I was 11, I started to see him less and less each month. I'd wake up on Saturday mornings hoping to see him that day, but most of the time I'd be disappointed. After about a year he called and asked Rob and me to spend weekends with him in New Jersey, where he was now living. Even though I was happy to be with him, I didn't show it that much. I was hurt because he had left us for so long.

The weekend stays at his house went so well that he asked us to spend that summer with him. I enjoyed that summer. He'd leave money on my pillow before he left for work in the morning. I looked forward to hearing his van pull up when he came home. I felt mad good because I had a dad again.

3. **Wedding Bells**

The year that followed was good because I saw him almost every weekend. Then one day my father picked up my brother and me and took us shopping in New Jersey. He bought us suits, shirts and ties and we went to his house in Newark, where he was living with a woman named Fay.

Suddenly my pops came into the living room, called my brother and me over into the corner, put his arms around us and said,

> **Despite his faults, I still admired my father.**

"We're going to a wedding on Saturday."

"Whose wedding?" I asked.

"Me and Fay's," he answered.

I had an idea that he'd say that. I was happy for him. I joined Fay's sons at the television, hoping to start a conversation because I really felt like I didn't belong. "Yo, you heard? Your moms and my pops are getting married," I said.

"We knew that for a year already. You just found out now?" Shawn asked.

I was embarrassed because my brother and I were the only people who hadn't known. I thought everyone was laughing at me.

"Now he has new sons and he doesn't need me anymore," I thought.

4. **Stepchild**

On the morning of the wedding, my brother and I helped decorate the hall where the ceremony and reception were to be held. It was hard work, but hours later the hall was transformed with tablecloths and decorations. I didn't mind doing all that work because I was looking forward to being a part of the wedding.

> **'What kind of father are you?' I asked him.**

But I didn't have anything to do with the ceremony. When it was over, I was still hoping to sit with my father, but I could have waited years for him to notice me. I was disappointed and upset. I felt as though my pops used me as his maid, as though I wasn't important to him.

After the wedding I spoke to my father only when it was absolutely necessary. As years raced by, the number of times that I saw him decreased.

I was angry at my pops for treating me like a stepchild at the wedding, but I still needed him in my life. It was very hard, and still is, to be a teen and my own father at the same time. I'd question whether I was good enough to be considered a man. I couldn't get through a day without stressing myself out about whether I acted, talked, or looked like a man. All that stress affected my life in many ways.

5. **The Confrontation**

Finally, about a year and a half ago, after years of keeping my feelings inside and many, many sessions talking with my counselor, I raised the courage to call him up and confront him.

"What kind of father are you?" I asked him. "You don't call, you don't come to see us. If anyone met me in the last two years, they'd think that I didn't have a father. I don't understand what's going on."

"Um, I have been calling and coming by," he said calmly.

"But you are never there."

The way he spoke to me made me feel like we were two executives at a meeting.

"You haven't been calling or coming 'cause I would've gotten a message," I said. "I think it's because you got your new sons and Karen [my older half-sister] over there, so you don't need us anymore."

I was hoping that he'd say that it wasn't true and that he still loved me, but that didn't happen.

"I don't think you should be taking this tone with me," he said. He was starting to get upset. "You call me up and tell me this bull about—"

"Bull?" I interrupted. "This ain't bull crap. It's the way I feel. I'm telling you the way I feel and that's all it is to you—bull crap!"

"OK, it's the way you feel. But I'm still your father and you shouldn't be speaking to me like this," he said.

"As far as I'm concerned, you're not my father. You haven't been and will never be my father," I told him.

"You will always be my son and we will be together in the future," he said in a patronizing voice.

"If you're not here for me now, what makes you think that I'm going to need you in the future?" I said. "Listen, I have another call so I gotta go, ah'ight." Click.

The conversation pissed me off. First, his tone made me feel like he wasn't taking me seriously. Second, he made me realize that I was right—he didn't want me.

But I felt a little relieved to at least know how he felt. Making that call was the hardest thing that I ever did. I was trembling while I was speaking to him. My emotions were so strong from keeping them in for so many years. It was good for me to get it out because now I don't think about him enough to get me depressed anymore.

6. **The Last Straw**

Surprisingly, he did call me back a few weeks later. He told me that he wanted to hang out with my brother and me that Friday. I canceled my plans so I could be with my dad.

At 7 o'clock on Friday night I was waiting for him. Nine o'clock came and I was getting frustrated. I finally decided to call and find out if something happened. Fay answered the phone and told me he was sleeping. She woke him up and he gave me some story about having a long day. Then he asked if he could see me on Sunday and I agreed.

> How can I love someone who I don't know and who doesn't know me?

To make a long story short, he never came on Sunday. From that day I realized that I was never going to have him in my life again. It is now March of '94 and I've neither seen nor heard from my father in more than a year.

7. **Mom Says I Should Love Him**

My mother still tries to convince me that I should love him because he's my father. But how can I love someone who I don't know and who doesn't know me?

Today things are better. I've managed to hide my feelings for my father so deep that I'd have to dig to find them. I still think he doesn't want me, but I don't care anymore. I realized that no matter what he did to me, it's no excuse for me to have a messed-up life. Strangely enough, he did teach me something.

He taught me that the best man I could be is his opposite. I now know that having children left and right doesn't make a man. Staying to raise them does. They say that when you get older you turn into your parents—I pray that doesn't happen to me.

Just the Two of Us

By Stephen Simpson

1.   "The Big Park," in the projects. A father and son playing basketball.

If you're watching from the sidelines, you can feel the competitiveness. The hard fouls, the shot-for-shot manner, the bragging with each basket. Even though you're not playing, the rivalry is there with you.

What's the score? 30-28. One basket could end the game.

"It's over, dad, this is my game."

"We'll see, just shoot the ball."

The son shoots and misses, and the father makes an easy put back to tie the score at 30-30.

"Game's 34 now," the father says with an "I'm gonna win" attitude. Two baskets later, game over; the father wins.

"Don't worry, Stephen, someday you'll beat me," he says with a laugh to his teary-eyed companion.

His words are followed by a hug and an Icy to enjoy on the way home. This is an everyday scene: two guys playing basketball. Except this bond is much deeper. This is the relationship I share with the only man I love: my father.

2. **My Role Model—My Father**

I believe that every boy or young man deserves a male role model or influence in his life. My role model goes by the name of Frederick Simpson Sr. I consider it a privilege to share a relationship with him, especially since some young men grow up and never meet or see their fathers.

I always tell my father that I want to be like him because of the way he carries himself and treats his children, and the way he lives his life. Some of my friends who don't have a father will come to him and talk to him. He gives them advice, plays with them and shows them the same love that he shows me.

Ever since I can remember, my father has taken time out to be with me, my brother and my sister. Even though he works two jobs, he doesn't let this interfere with the family.

He does this because he never had a tight relationship with his father, so he tries to give us all the love and attention we need.

3. **My Folks Are Strict**

I also talk with my mother, but she doesn't have that kind of "guy" connection I have with my father, you know? Still, my mother has also influenced me in ways my father can't.

She teaches me etiquette because she wants me to be a gentleman (I am), she teaches me how to treat women because (come on, you know!), and, most of all, she teaches me independence because following the crowd almost never pays off. I think she's responsible for the softer, quiet side of me.

I love my parents for instilling their wisdom in me, and for letting me know clearly what is right and wrong. My parents laid down the laws for our house a long time ago. Their rules are:

1) They are the authority (like it or not).
2) Don't ever be afraid to bring anything to them.
3) Go to school and do well.
(There are some others, but I don't want to write a book.)

4. **Arguments—and Help**

I know my parents have lived longer and seen it all, so they usually have the answers for my problems. And my father will always pull us (me, my brother, sister or friends) aside if we're falling off track.

To me, that shows that he cares about us, because if he didn't, he wouldn't bother to say anything. If I am making my relationship with my parents seem perfect, I'm not trying to. (It's not!)

I have had quite a few problems with my folks. For example, when I began my sophomore year of high school, just about all I did was cut. We argued a lot over my report card grades that year. And my parents get mad when my attitude shows up in a conversation, or when I do something wrong and I don't want to admit it.

5. Trusting Parents, Not Friends

But I guess I trust that my parents are right about most things because I saw what happened to my brother when he stopped listening to them.

My brother was "numero uno" in our house for years, but he decided that he wanted to be with his friends more than family. In high school, he became rebellious and didn't listen to them about anything anymore.

I can't totally explain what happened to my brother, but he started to listen to the advice of his friends more than the advice of his parents. He ended up dropping out of high school and getting kicked out of the house.

> **Every boy or young man deserves a male role model or influence in his life.**

I messed up in school from 2nd all the way up to 5th grade. I'm not sure why I messed up. Maybe it was just because I didn't like school (I still don't).

But whatever it was, it got my parents really mad at me. They calmly explained (not!) that talking and fooling around in class is not the way school works. That discussion helped start my 180 degree turnaround in school.

6. Stepping in the Right Direction

What triggered the turnaround? Well, believe it or not, the way that my parents used to come down on me made me see that life doesn't mean anything if you fail.

It didn't happen overnight (see above), but I gradually started to take steps in the right direction. Another factor in the turn-around was that I basically got sick of getting beatings for bad report cards. My father stresses both discipline and compassion; and I love my father, but I couldn't stand it when he used to beat me.

Those words, "Stephen, I'm going to beat you," never failed to strike fear in my heart. I deserved a beating, but no kid likes parental discipline. He doesn't do it anymore (thank heaven), but he had his reasons when I was younger.

> My father isn't just tough, though. He also loves to hug and kiss, which can be embarrassing.

Many people today mistake discipline for abuse. I think reprimanding your children when they're wrong is not abuse. If you take that discipline out of context, then that is abuse. My parents never abused me with their discipline, but their correction has helped me stay on the right path.

7. Tough Love

My father has always tried to keep us from making the same mistakes he made as a child, like not going to college. He was smart enough to do anything, but no one encouraged him. I think that is why he encourages us to do well in school.

"I never had anyone behind me like we're behind you, Stephen," my parents often tell me. My father wants me to move on to better things. No one in the family has gone to college yet.

My father isn't just tough, though. He also loves to hug and kiss, which can be embarrassing. He's also very playful, so it doesn't take much to get him started. He is very open, so you can often find us sitting talking. He tells me about when he was my age, about life, and a good joke every now and then. I talk to him (and my mother) about all my problems, my achievements and my life.

8. A Real Man Isn't Macho

My father stresses how to be a man. Nowadays, when boys think being a man is having a baby or having sex with lots of girls, he tells us that a real man would care for the baby he made and doesn't need to hit "anything in a skirt."

Sometimes me and my boys will act too macho (sometimes if we see a girl, we start hooting, hollering and flexing our muscles), but he'll pull us aside and tell us it doesn't take all that.

My father gives good advice. And I love that he will always tell me, my brother, sister and my mother that he loves us.

He says it any time, when we're playing around, before he leaves for work, "Just so we'll know."

Learning to Forgive

By Christopher B.

1.   Every time I would see my mother we would always argue. She would bring up things that happened in the past and throw them in my face. I found it hard to forgive her for the problems we had in the past that led me to end up in juvenile prison. My social worker, Ms. Davis, knew my relationship with my mother was not good and urged me to go to therapy. Ms. Davis wanted to see us get along better.

I didn't want to go to any "stupid" therapy to talk about the problems I had with my mother. I felt I would be wasting my time, because my relationship with her wasn't going to get better.

Ms. Davis told me I had to go to therapy because it was part of my "service plan" while I was in the system. I felt like I was being forced to do something I didn't want to do. But I finally decided to go to therapy because I didn't want to end up going to another group home.

2. ### Afraid to Trust

I started going to therapy on Saturdays. Ms. Smith was the name of my therapist. I could see that she had a nice personality from the way she spoke to the kids and their mothers. We spoke briefly in her office for the first time. She was very patient and I felt comfortable talking to her. She explained that she wasn't going to try to rush me into expressing myself about my problems with my mother. She wanted me to get to know her better before I started confiding in her.

I didn't like talking about my problems with anybody. I felt like I couldn't trust anybody. I had been hurt a lot by many loved ones who were supposed to be in my corner when times got rough. They let me down big time by misusing the trust I had in them.

By going to therapy each week, I started to express myself better. I took my time telling Ms. Smith about my problems to see if I could trust her. I told her it was going to be difficult forgiving my mother because I was still carrying so much anger.

3. **A Mother's Anger**

My mother always tried to call me at the group home. I would tell the staff that I didn't want to speak to her. She would leave messages for me to call her. I didn't want to have anything to do with her. I had been making it without her, so why did I need her now? When I saw her on the streets, I would walk past her without saying anything.

The reason why things got this bad between us was because my mother treated me the same way my father treated her. My father mentally abused my mother. He would always try to belittle her every time they argued. I always felt my mother acted out her anger towards me because my father treated her badly. I always found it harder to get along with her than my sisters did. She always treated me differently from them. She went shopping with them and spent time with them. I reacted by spending a lot of time away from home to avoid her.

> **I didn't want to go to any 'stupid' therapy to talk about the problems I had with my mother.**

When I went to therapy one Saturday, Ms. Smith wanted me to talk about what happened to cause me to end up in a detention center. I told Ms. Smith that one night my mother and I got in a huge fight when I came home very late and disrespected her by talking back to her. I told her that my mother got real upset and that she tried to hit me with a chair. When I blocked it with my hands, the chair fell back on top of her. She then tried to hit me on the head with a glass vase. My sister's boyfriend got in front of me and blocked her swing with his hands. My mother cut his hands so badly that he had to go to the hospital for 100 stitches.

I started getting upset while I was telling my therapist what happened to me. She stopped me for a minute so I could calm myself down. I was very emotional and frustrated while talking about my problems.

When we continued, I told Ms. Smith how my mother came to court and accused me of cutting my sister's boyfriend with a piece of glass. She also told the court how I hit her with a chair and how she had to go to the doctor. I was locked up in a New York City jail for two weeks before going upstate for one and a half years. I felt one and a half years were taken away from me for no reason.

4. The First Step

Ms. Smith told me that I had to learn how to forgive and release the pain inside me. She said the first step in forgiving someone is to really mean it from the heart. I heard what she said but I didn't know if I was ready to make that first step. I didn't know if I was ready to open up my heart to my mother and forgive her.

> I had been hurt a lot by many loved ones who were supposed to be in my corner when times got rough.

I left therapy that day feeling like a better person. I finally got the chance to release some anger by talking about my problems. During my ride on the train I was thinking about my mother and what Ms. Smith said about forgiving. I knew everybody makes mistakes and they deserve a second chance.

5. A New Understanding

My mother called me around 7 o'clock that same night. Lisa, one of the staff workers, asked me if I wanted to speak to her. I took the phone and I told her that we needed to talk things out.

My mother agreed and she sounded very good. She wanted me to come to the house after school.

I went to see my mother the next day. I wanted to talk to her about the problems that we had. I realized as I got older that I was at fault for some of the problems because I never listened to anybody and I wanted things to be done my way. I had to stop feeling sorry for myself because I ended up in a detention center. I wanted to tell her how sorry I was that I didn't listen to her, and that I disrespected her by coming home any time I felt like when I was living with her. I wanted to tell her how I felt about her as a mother, and how I wanted to start a new relationship as mother and son.

She was cooking dinner for my two sisters when I walked in the kitchen. My mother asked me how I was doing in school and in my group home. I was nervous to be under the same roof with her, because this was the first time in two years that I was able to come home to visit. I didn't want the same thing to happen as when the cops had to remove me from my house. I went into my big sister's room to talk with her until my mother was finished cooking dinner.

My mother called me from my sister's room to have dinner and talk with her alone at the table. She told me how sorry she was for coming to court and seeing me end up in juvenile detention. She said she was hurt by the way I was treating her that night. I told my mother that I forgave her and I wanted to start a new relationship with her and just move on.

6. Better Communication

I could see tears running down her cheeks when she told me I was the only son that God gave her and she loved me tremendously. I stood up to hug my mother because I knew she really meant every word she said.

My relationship with my mother is much better than it has been in the past. We are able to communicate better and get along well. I can go to the house anytime I want and eat. I can go home on weekend passes and I spend all the major holidays with her.

The reason why our relationship has changed is because we both realize that everybody makes mistakes and deserves a second chance. I had to realize that I couldn't just blame my mother for what she did. If I had listened to her when she told me to come in the house early, she would have never been put in a situation of being worried and angry about my disobedience.

7. Therapy Helped

I'm glad my relationship with my mother has gotten much better, but we still have problems. I'm able to deal with them better and talk about them without holding any negative feelings inside. If it wasn't for therapy, my relationship with my mother would still be the same. I just wanted her to love me the same way she loved my two sisters.

My mother and I started going to therapy together to try to prevent what happened in the past from ever happening again. It was hard being in therapy with her because I was afraid that she was going to get mad if I said something she didn't like. My mother is the type of person who gets offended easily and is not afraid to defend herself. When I was in therapy alone it was easier to express myself and the room was less tense, but eventually I got used to being in therapy with her. We spoke about the problems we had in the past. I felt wonderful on the inside because we were able to communicate and be in the same room together.

> **I want to take it slow in developing a good relationship with my mother.**

I feel our relationship is better, but I wouldn't want to destroy it by rushing home before I'm ready.

I want to take it slow in developing a good relationship with my mother. But if something terrible happened to her health and she needed me at home to take care of her, I wouldn't even think twice about packing my bags and going to be by her side. I love her with all my heart, even though we had a lot of problems in the past.

Summer of Secrets

By Paul Langan

"I can't do this again, Carl. I don't have the strength, not without Mama."

Darcy Wills hid in the dark hallway listening to the sound of her mother's weary voice. It was 11:00 at night, and Mom was in the bedroom talking with Dad. Their door was closed. But through the thin walls of her family's small house, Darcy could hear them as if they were standing right in front of her.

"So what are you trying to say?" Dad asked. His voice was strained, as if he was carrying a heavy block of cement on his back.

Darcy stood still as a statue, careful not to make a sound that would alert her parents to the fact that she was just a few feet away in the dark.

"I don't know, Carl," Mom answered. "I don't know anything anymore."

There was a moment of silence, and Darcy thought she heard her mother sob.

"I just don't have a good feeling about any of this."

So it *was* true, Darcy thought. Something was definitely wrong with her parents. Darcy had sensed it for days. She had noticed tension between them and had even heard Mom snap a few times, but until now she figured her mother was still recovering from the loss of Grandma.

This is Chapter 1 from Summer of Secrets by Paul Langan in the Bluford Series. Copyright 2004 © by Townsend Press. Reprinted with permission. www.townsendpress.com

Only three weeks ago, after a slow, steady decline in her health, Grandma had died in her sleep in the bedroom at the end of the hallway. The loss left a depressing void in the house. But in the three weeks that had passed, the sadness was replaced by an uncomfortable silence, one Darcy couldn't understand.

"Just don't worry about it, Darce," said her sister Jamee last week. Jamee was fourteen, two years younger than Darcy. "Anyway, it's none of your business. Besides, Mom's tough, and Dad's here. They'll be okay."

Darcy had rolled her eyes at her sister's comment. Jamee wasn't the best person to judge a situation. Only six months ago, she had dated Bobby Wallace, a sixteen-year-old who messed with drugs, hit Jamee, and convinced her to shoplift for him.

"How can you be so sure?" Darcy had asked.

Jamee shrugged off the question. "You know what your problem is, Darcy? You think too much," she said and then left to go to the movies with her friend Cindy Gibson. It was what Jamee always did when anything serious confronted her. Run away. Hide. Ignore it. Anything to avoid things that were unpleasant or difficult. It was Jamee's way, not Darcy's.

No, the problem is that you don't think enough, Darcy thought as she watched her sister leave. No matter what Jamee said, Darcy knew the issue with her parents was serious. For weeks, Mom had walked around in a daze, sometimes, it seemed, on the verge of tears.

Yesterday, Darcy even spotted her watching what she hated most—a TV show about a hospital emergency room. For as long as Darcy could remember, Mom had forbidden all medical shows when she was around.

"I see that stuff every day at work. I'm not going to watch it when I'm home," she had once declared. Mom was an emergency room nurse. Though she rarely discussed what she saw at the hospital, Darcy knew that her mother witnessed victims of shootings, stabbings, car accidents, and all sorts of diseases. No wonder she didn't want to see it on TV. But last night, she did not even seem to notice the TV doctors trying to revive a patient who had a heart attack. It was as if her mind was somewhere else. As if she wasn't in the room, even though her body was sprawled across the couch.

But tonight, Mom was even worse. Her face looked worn when she came home from the hospital. It wasn't the usual tiredness that made her stretch out on the couch and sleep after she got home. It was deeper, as if Mom's spirit was drained like an old battery.

"Are you all right?" Darcy had asked as Mom came in the front door, slumped onto the living room sofa, and sighed. She had not even said hello to Dad, who was making dinner for her in the kitchen.

"I'm fine," Mom grumbled. Her voice had a hollow sound to it, as if she didn't believe her own words.

Darcy was certain her parents were having serious problems. That had to be why Mom was acting so strange. The last time Darcy had witnessed her parents fighting was when she was in middle school, just before her father left. There was the same tension in the house then, the same awkward silence.

"Are you sure you're okay, Mom?" Darcy had asked, hoping her mother would explain what was bothering her. Darcy couldn't help remembering the August day years ago when Dad took her and Jamee out for ice cream. She recalled the pained look on his face and the heavy drag of his steps on the concrete. It was the last thing he did with them before he took off, before the five-year span without a phone call, a birthday card, or a single word.

Mom cried every night for a month when Dad left. Seeing her so upset was almost worse than losing Dad. It was a kind of torture that made Darcy shudder whenever she remembered it. Only Grandma's strength enabled Mom to work full-time, pay the bills, and hold the family together. Now Grandma was gone, and Darcy knew that if her parents split up again, there would be no one for Mom to turn to.

"Yes, I'm sure!" Mom snapped. "I'm just tired. You understand? And you know the one thing that bothers me most when I'm tired? It's people asking me what's wrong."

"Sorry," Darcy said, stepping back. She had not expected Mom to get so angry. It was just more proof that there were major problems in the family.

For the rest of the evening, Mom didn't say a word, even when Jamee came home a half hour late from the movies.

"Cindy's mom was late picking us up," Jamee explained as soon as she walked in.

Darcy did not believe her sister. There was something rehearsed about what she said, as if she had practiced it a few times. But Mom didn't even acknowledge Jamee, who quickly grabbed the cordless phone from the kitchen and retreated into her room.

For two hours, except for the TV, everything was unnaturally quiet. But Darcy knew it was a false calm, like the muffled silence just before a bad storm.

As soon as her parents headed into the bedroom, Darcy turned out the lights, locked the doors, and crept into the hallway to find out what was wrong. Now she stood outside her parents' bedroom, trying to catch pieces of their private conversation.

"What can I say to make you feel better about this?" Dad said. Darcy could feel the strain in his voice. He was upset.

"There's nothing you can say," Mom replied. "I'm too old for this, and I don't want to be in this situation. I just can't do it again, Carl. I just can't."

Suddenly Jamee's bedroom door opened, and she stepped into the hallway. Darcy turned and tried to act as if she was walking toward her own bedroom.

"What are you doing?" Jamee whispered, nearly running into Darcy.

"Just going to bed."

"No you're not. You're listening to Mom and Dad, aren't you?"

"*No*," Darcy whispered. "And keep your voice down."

"Darcy, you're the worst liar. Even in the dark, I can tell you aren't telling the truth. Why don't you just leave them alone?"

"Because something is wrong, Jamee. I know it. They didn't say a word to each other at dinner tonight, and even you had to notice that Mom's been out of it. I'm just worried."

"Maybe she's just in a bad mood or something," Jamee said, but her whisper cracked. Darcy could see Jamee's eyes dart back and forth in the darkness. She was shaking her head the way she always did when she was upset.

Though Jamee talked tough, Darcy knew that her younger sister looked up to Dad more than anyone in the world. Jamee would take it harder than anyone if Mom and Dad were having problems.

"I hope that's all it is, Jamee," Darcy said, though she was sure it wasn't. And she suspected Jamee felt the same way.

Jamee walked into the kitchen, hung up the phone she had grabbed earlier, and poured herself a glass of water. Darcy followed her.

"Why can't things just be easy for once?" Jamee said, leaning against the kitchen wall.

The two were silent for a second. Darcy wished Grandma was there to talk to. Or that Hakeem, her ex-boyfriend, was somewhere nearby so she could call him. But Grandma was gone, dead from a massive stroke, and Hakeem was living in Detroit, far away from their crowded neighborhood in southern California.

"I don't wanna think about something bad happening with Mom and Dad. I just can't deal with that," Jamee confessed between sips of water.

"Like you said. Maybe it's not that bad," Darcy replied, trying to keep her sister's spirits up.

"Yeah right," Jamee whispered bitterly. "When are things around here ever better than you expected?"

Before Darcy could reply, her sister turned and walked out of the kitchen. "I'm going to bed," Jamee said as she left. A second later, her bedroom door closed with a soft thud.

Darcy stood at the edge of the dark hallway and listened.

The house was deathly quiet, as if everything had been swept under a heavy blanket of gloom. Reluctantly, she decided to go to bed too.

Lying in bed, Darcy stared at the shadowy ceiling of her room, unable to relax. It was so quiet she could hear the rhythmic click of her watch on the other side of the room.

Tick tick tick. Like the heartbeat of some unwanted guest.

Darcy's body was tired from a full day of work at Scoops, the new ice cream parlor not far from Bluford High, where she had just finished her sophomore year. But her mind was wide awake, as if she had just drunk ten cups of coffee.

It had been this way for days, even before she noticed the strange tension between her parents. As soon as it got quiet and she was ready to go to sleep, Darcy would remember the afternoon weeks ago, when she was attacked by Brian Mason.

Often the memory was so strong, it was as if he was in the room with her, pinning her down, threatening her again, making her heart race with fear.

"What's wrong with you?" Brian's words still insulted her, bouncing inside her mind like ricocheting bullets. When he attacked, Darcy had struggled to free herself, but Brian's grip was strong, like a vise crushing her arm. Sometimes, she still felt the pain from where he had pinned her against the couch in his apartment.

"Stop it!" she had demanded. "Let me go."

It had been a nightmare that caught Darcy completely off guard. She had met Brian just before summer vacation began when she babysat for his sister, Liselle. At first, he seemed nice, and for a time, Darcy was flattered by his attention, especially after her old boyfriend, Hakeem Randall, broke up with her. On the day of the attack, Brian invited her to spend time alone with him, and she agreed, lying to her parents so they would let her out. But once she got there, Brian started getting physical with her. Too physical.

"You're acting like a baby," Brian had yelled when Darcy tried to stop him from lifting up her shirt.

Darcy could still feel him gripping her, his wet lips pushing against her neck, his roving hands. His musky smell. On that afternoon, he had touched her more than any other boy, even Hakeem.

No one except Mom and Dad knew of the attack. Not Jamee. Not Hakeem. Not even Tarah Carson, Darcy's best friend. It was a secret, an invisible scar Darcy faced alone each night.

If Dad hadn't shown up...

Darcy could not bear the thought, yet she couldn't escape it either. She knew the dark corner it went to. It was the same conclusion every night.

In fifth grade, just before Dad left, Darcy had gotten into a fight at school with a seventh grade boy who pulled her bra strap, making it snap painfully against her back. To the kid, it was just a joke. But Dad had seen what happened, grabbed the boy and dragged him to the principal's office.

"What's wrong with you, boy? You treat girls with respect, you hear me!" Dad had yelled, holding the kid's shirt in his clenched fist. Even the principal looked scared.

It was then Darcy knew her father would always keep her safe. Would protect her when she needed it. Would never allow anyone to hurt her. Dad had proved that again when Brian attacked. He had saved her. He had stopped Brian from going any further. He had found her and brought her home.

But now, with her parents fighting, it seemed Dad might not always be there. Maybe he would go away again, perhaps for good.

Darcy trembled in her bed.

If Dad hadn't shown up...

If Dad wasn't there...

If Dad leaves again...

Darcy's mind raced, as it had each night for the past week. In the shadows, she could almost feel the specter of Brian watching her. And even though she knew he was gone, that he had moved over 300 miles away to Oakland to live with his aunt, Darcy still could not shake the damage he had done, the crack he had put in her world, one that left voices deep inside her which she could not silence.

"*You're not safe,*" the voices said. "*Boys can't be trusted. The world is dangerous. Your father won't always be there to protect you.*"

You can read the rest of this story in Summer of Secrets, *by Paul Langan.*

REAL TOUGH
Dealing With Difficult Situations

My Secret Addiction

By Christina G.

1.   I first cut myself when I was 13.

I was feeling depressed and dead inside. I noticed a box of razor blades lying on the kitchen shelf. I took a blade from the box and took it to my room.

I closed the door. I thought for a minute, and then made a half-inch cut on my left wrist. At first I felt nothing, as usual. Then came the pain—like a paper cut—and the feeling that a door had been opened. My heart beat really fast. I felt a rush. I felt powerful, and alive.

Two drops of bright blood appeared. I squeezed and scratched to make the cut bleed more. After about two more drops, the bleeding stopped. Then I went to lie down, and come down from the rush. I felt guilty about what I'd done.

But a week later I tried it again. Though it may seem hard to understand, it felt good to feel something after feeling nothing for so long. Cutting soon became a regular part of my life.

2. **Scared of School**

My problems began back in elementary school. I was extremely shy; too afraid to go to school. At first it was the building itself I couldn't enter. Then, once I was inside the building, I couldn't go into my classroom. I would become paralyzed at the door.

In junior high, I used to sit in the stairwell and cry. Lots of days I'd skip school completely. I'd stay home and watch television, read, write and play.

After a while I began to hate myself—the school situation, my weight and my shyness. I began not to care about the way I dressed, or if I got dressed in the morning at all. I'd sleep half the day. I almost never went out.

3. Adults Called Me Crazy

All along, adults called me crazy. In elementary school, one social worker even told me I belonged in the psychiatric ward of the hospital.

My junior high principal said that if I didn't go to class I would be taken away from my house and locked up. He once dragged me down the hall crying, and pushed me into my classroom. He told my class that I had "psychological problems." I ran out of that school and never returned.

Everyone tried to take control of my life and find out what was "wrong" with me. I was sent to a therapist against my will. They tried to push me and guide me, but they only succeeded in backing me further into the corner I was in. I began to trust only myself and became even more depressed.

> I was alone. The only person I had was myself.

By the time I was 13, I was growing more and more apathetic. The first therapist I ever liked had left, and I got shifted to a woman who I hated almost as much as I hated myself.

4. I Kept My Cuts to Myself

That's when I started cutting myself. In the beginning I usually just made one cut at a time, every few days or so. But after awhile I began to make more cuts. By the time I was 14, I was doing it several times a day, and sometimes I'd even slash myself many times in hidden places like my chest.

Most of the cuts were in places where I figured no one would ever see or think that it was on purpose. I could claim cutting my fingers was from paper cuts. (I guess there was also a little vanity, because I never cut myself too deep in places where I didn't want scars.)

5. Pain Equaled Power

But sometimes I would open my cuts up again and make them bleed more, or poke at them with a pin or needle, all to feel more pain. Other times I'd only drag the blade across my skin just to feel the coldness and a slight burn.

Pain was something real; it was a way for me to jar my feelings, good and bad, back from wherever they had gone. I could turn to the pain whenever I wanted to. There I had ultimate power.

After I cut myself, though, I'd feel guilty about what I'd done. I wondered why I had done it, and when my emotional pain and emptiness would end. I decided that killing myself was the answer. I didn't have any other control in my life, so death seemed a good option.

6. Feeling Dead Inside

Trying to kill myself didn't work the first time, and I felt like such a worthless failure that I slashed myself many times. I tried several more times over the next year and a half. After each time, I felt really bad and cut myself. Cutting had become a way to both help and punish myself. It helped me feel something again, but also became a way for me to take out my self-hatred.

I couldn't tell anyone about what I was doing. I was afraid if anyone found out they would judge me and I would get locked up.

I knew my family would only make me feel worse. I didn't have any friends because I'd lost them all when I stopped going to school. I couldn't tell my therapist because I knew she was required by law to report it.

On top of all that, I fiercely guarded my privacy, so throwing myself out into the spotlight and having to face probing questions was not something I was willing to do.

I was alone. The only person I had was myself.

7. Going Back to School

Two years ago, I was finally able to go to school again on a regular basis.

It isn't easy for me to explain what changed. School staff had tried everything to get me back in school. They put me in special ed, held me back a year, and changed my school. They even tried to send a teacher to my house.

But I didn't want any of that. So I enrolled in high school. After a week of trying, I was finally able to enter the classroom. Though it wasn't easy at first, I began to attend classes regularly. When I got more involved in school, I began to talk to other teens about my experiences.

8. Trapped in a Blue Month

Some said that I was crazy and needed "serious psychological" help; others could understand because they'd done it too.

Last year, a friend and I were sitting in a locker bay after lunch. I was still getting used to going to school and being around my peers, but I was in a very blue month.

My friend and I were sitting there talking and laughing, but I felt really bad. So I broke the tab off of my soda can and began scratching at my wrist with it. He grabbed my arm and took the tab away from me, but I stood up, ripped the can open and used that instead. My scratches were swelling a little and burning. He pleaded with me to give him the can, which I did.

I felt like hell afterwards. I felt guilty, and ashamed of having done it in front of another person for the first time. I just sat on the floor, silent, wanting to cry and disappear.

Taking Control

9.

That's when I decided I wanted to stop cutting myself. I began to take control of my life. I started applying myself completely in school and doing well. I also stopped going to the therapist who I didn't like.

I made many friends, and started going out and doing more things. I began to say what I wanted and to do what I wanted. I began to get things for myself.

Once I started experiencing life and improving it, my feelings about cutting changed. Before, cutting seemed like a way to get control. Now, cutting myself seemed like a loss of control. It had lost its importance and meaning. I no longer needed to do that because I was no longer stuck in a rut.

Because people weren't pushing me anymore I had freedom to expand on my own. Probably most important, I didn't feel like the walking dead any longer. I stopped cutting myself and eventually stopped feeling suicidal.

10. **Capable and Happy**

There were times when I was tempted to do it again, like when I felt bad after my boyfriend broke up with me. But I didn't do it because I could be OK without hurting myself.

I had already come through a ton of stuff and the end of that relationship was actually one of the things that taught me that I wasn't a weak person, and that I was capable of doing anything and being happy.

> **Like everyone else, I have my highs and lows, but they don't affect me like they used to.**

It's been about a year and a half since the last time I cut myself. There was no magic involved in stopping, it just took time.

When I got over my fear of school, many doors opened. I think that the rest all happened from there. It wasn't until everyone really backed off and gave me my space that I was finally able to figure things out for myself and fix my life.

These days I am truly happy for the first time. Like everyone else, I have my highs and lows, but they don't affect me like they used to. Now, I love to have new experiences.

This spring, a friend who was upset by all of his tests and

schoolwork asked me what there is to live for. I told him there is a lot to live for.

"This from the formerly suicidal," I said. We laughed and continued walking.

I Could Have Been Elisa

By James Knight

1.   I am a 20-year-old male who practically grew up in foster care. I went into the system at the age of 7 and I'm still in it. I am angered by the senseless death of 6-year-old Elisa Izquierdo, which I heard about on TV. She was tortured to death by her mother.

New York City and State authorities, including the Child Abuse Hotline, were notified many times that Elisa was being abused, but she was never taken from her home. My siblings and I lived in an abusive foster home, suffering many of the same things as Elisa did, yet no one heard our cries for help either.

My four siblings and I were taken away from our natural mother and placed together in several foster homes. We were innocent children, but we thought it was our fault we were taken away.

The foster mother (who eventually was allowed to adopted us!) was an emotionally unstable woman who disliked children, but was still given a license to provide and care for them.

2. No Mercy

She often told us that she took us in for the money. She always said she couldn't care less about us, as long as her bills were paid.

She beat us with any object she could get her hands on, and she never had mercy for our faces. She beat us with a thick cow-hide belt which she slit into seven strips. She called the belt "Mr. Brown." My siblings and I had welts on our bare skin for days due to the beatings. We were also beaten with pots and pans, a wooden brush, hangers, broomsticks and her fists.

Every time we yelled at the top of our voices for help, she turned up the radio so no one could hear our cries. Elisa's mother also turned up the radio.

A stray dog should not have been placed in the care of my adoptive mother. We were treated as if we didn't have any feelings or importance. She watched as we bathed, even telling us what parts of our bodies to wash. We weren't allowed to tell her how ashamed and embarrassed we felt. We were stripped of our pride and dignity.

> **I was afraid no one would believe I was being abused.**

There were many nights we went to bed hungry. She felt we didn't deserve to eat because we were "bad." We didn't have a normal childhood. We couldn't play or do any of the things other children do.

When you're told every day of your life that you're never going to amount to anything, it puts a painful strain on the mind and heart. I believed the harsh words she said because she was an adult.

3. Case Dismissed

No matter how much we begged and pleaded to the child welfare services, police officers and the Child Abuse Hotline, no one reached out to help us. For example, when I was 11 or 12 years old I called the hotline and a man assured me they would look into my case.

I felt relieved, knowing I was not alone. A social worker arrived the next day. My adoptive mother denied the abuse.

The social worker then asked us—with my adoptive mother right in the room—if we were being abused. Since we were terrified of our mother, of course we said no.

The case was immediately dismissed. We felt helpless and trapped. We had nobody to turn to.

When we ran away from home, a police officer took us back and said, "You kids have it made living here. This is a clean home with plenty of food in the refrigerator, and a loving mother to provide for you. You kids are crazy not wanting to stay here." As soon as the officer left, the beatings continued where they had left off.

4. **Putting On an Act**

The police officer never asked us how we felt or what we were going through in that hellhole. Our scars from her beatings didn't make a difference to him. He acted as if we deserved the beatings. His only concern was to bring us back home. He took the word of our abuser since she was an adult with a kind appearance and a clean house with plenty of food in the refrigerator.

My adoptive mother was a totally different person in the presence of the police. She would put on an act that looked so natural. She would give the police coffee and donuts and then she would show them her immaculate (spotless) house—that my siblings and I had cleaned.

The naked eye can be very deceiving. You can see things you only want to see. While riding in the back seat of the police car, I often heard the officers mumble, "Damn, we gotta go through all this paperwork from these kids' nonsense." I strongly believe the officer felt his job would be easier if he ignored our pleas for help.

5. **Denying the Abuse**

No one saw the physical and emotional pain Elisa Izquierdo carried every day of her life. Those who did see it chose not to get involved, and when others tried, the proper authorities didn't take action.

People must realize children are terrified of telling someone that they're being abused. I went to school many days with cuts and bruises on my face. My teachers often asked what happened, and I would always say I fell or tripped over my shoelaces. I was afraid no one would believe I was being abused.

I eventually left the abuse by refusing to go back home, and when I was 14 I was finally signed into a new foster home. My siblings stayed years longer with my adoptive mother and only recently left her home.

If you suspect a child is being abused, report it without any hesitation. I know most people do not want to get involved. For example, some of our neighbors heard the beatings we received, but didn't want to report it. Years later, they told me they felt it was none of their business. But someone has to take a stand to save the lives of innocent children.

Remember, it is not the children's fault that they're being abused.

Parents, talk to your child instead of beating him or her. Trust me—it really works. I know it's hard to have patience, but what do you have to lose by not beating your child? Also remember— your child is a part of you.

Based on my experiences, I feel there's a great need for the system to make drastic changes in order to save the lives of innocent and abused children.

6. Need for Changes

■ *Child care workers should talk to children outside of the home when there is a suspicion of abuse. A child is more comfortable revealing abuse outside the home and away from adults. My siblings and I couldn't reveal the abuse in front of our adoptive mother.*

■ *Interview the children separately. Children will be more honest if interviewed separately. They won't feel the pressure from a sibling to hide the abuse. This will also prevent one sibling from snitching to the abuser about what another child said.*

■ *Social workers, when they make visits, must help the children feel safe. A child is more likely to be frightened by someone they don't know. In my case, the social worker didn't make us feel comfortable when she asked us questions.*

■ *Social workers and child care workers should make surprise visits to check on allegations of abuse. Letting the person know you're coming by isn't an effective way to investigate the home.*

■ *Screen foster parents more thoroughly. My adoptive mother should never have been approved as a foster parent.*

■ *Increase the budget for foster care. A lack of well-trained and well-paid social workers and caseworkers in the system will only lead to more children being abused.*

Elisa didn't have a chance to fulfill her hopes and dreams. Maybe she would have become a teacher, a mother, or a nurse. Now she can't be any of those things.

This story was very painful to write because it brought back so many horrible memories, but I have to keep in mind how lucky and thankful I am to be alive and well. I see myself as a survivor, not a victim. I wish Elisa Izquierdo could feel the same way.

Chinese Parents, American Me

By Ngan-Fong Huang

1.   About a year ago, I went to the Village and bought a pair of blue, baggy jeans and a long shirt that I buttoned only at the top. When my mom saw my new outfit, she shouted, "Look at your jeans! They're too wide and too long for you."

I just stared at her, shocked by her reaction.

"They're sagging from your waist and scraping on the ground," she continued. "What are you trying to be? Like those gangsters whose jeans hang so low that they nearly fall to the ground?"

About a week later I tried the jeans on again and noticed that they seemed a lot shorter. I immediately looked at the hemline and saw strands of blue thread sticking out. I realized that my mom had secretly snuck into my room, searched my closet for the jeans, cut a few inches off the bottoms, and then sewed them back up.

2. How Dare You!

I was furious. I stormed into her room and asked, "Why did you cut off the bottoms of my jeans? They were mine! How could you do this without asking me?"

"I told you they were too long," was all she said.

"Now I'll never wear these jeans again!" I yelled. "I'll get new ones."

You can call me the typical American-born Chinese (ABC). Like most immigrants, my parents came here for a better future—for them and for my sisters and me. But I often feel torn between the ways of my parents and those of the society in which I grew up. On one hand, I want to be accepted by my friends as an American.

On the other hand, my parents want me to maintain our traditions. Not knowing what to do, I try to find a middle ground.

When I was little, I was comfortable thinking of myself only as Chinese. I had always been sheltered by my family and had not had much contact with other cultures. It was only in kindergarten that I began opening my eyes to all the different people around me.

3. **The Only Asian on the Block**

Because there were no other Chinese families in the neighborhood, all my friends were either Hispanic or African-American. They could not speak Chinese, did not know what the Moon Festival was, or even about the days when we honor our deceased ancestors. I felt very lonely being the only Asian.

I wanted to be accepted. I wanted to be just like my friends. So I did the only logical thing I could do—I too began to idolize Bugs Bunny and Big Bird. I played with the same kinds of Barbie dolls, and even played yard games like tag and hopscotch just like they did. And my friends finally began to accept me.

> **I felt very lonely being the only Asian.**

But no matter how I tried to fit in, I always knew I was different from them. I was not a true American. My straight, dark brown hair and almond-shaped eyes looked different from my friends' light, curly hair and large, round eyes. My eyelashes didn't curl up the way theirs did either.

That December, one of my friends asked me, "What presents are you getting from Santa this year?"

4. **Santa Who?**

I was confused. Earlier that year I had learned about a jolly, white-bearded Santa who flew into the air with reindeer, stuffing presents into the socks of sleeping children on the night of

Christmas Eve. My parents had never mentioned him to me before. As far as I knew, Chinese New Year was the most festive occasion of the year, not Christmas. I didn't know how to respond but finally answered, "No, we don't celebrate Christmas."

My friend looked at me shocked, as if I was the most deprived child in the world.

Growing up, television sitcoms like *Full House* and *Leave It to Beaver* made me feel even more like I was not a real American. By the time I was 8 years old, I could already see how the children in the television shows had such open relationships with their parents. They could ask them for advice about anything— school, even about boyfriends. The teenagers were free to stay out late, could dress however they wanted and were not pressured to get good grades. Best of all, the family members always hugged and forgave each other.

> I have tried to make my parents see that I am mature enough to control my own life.

5. **Torn Between Two Traditions**

That was not how my family was. There were no hugs or any signs of affection at all. For us it was just supposed to be inferred. And even now, at the age of 17, I would never even think about talking to either of my parents about dating because I know they do not approve of it at this age. Life in my family is more about school and grades, not relationships. My parents also think that girls should dress conservatively—no miniskirts, tank tops, or other clothing that shows more skin than just the arms, face and legs below the knees.

Often I feel very confused because I cannot decide whether to go on obeying my parents or do what I feel is right for me. To deal with this problem, I have tried to make my parents see that I am mature enough to control my own life. They may be upset and nag me for coming home later than 7 p.m., for example. But I try to convince them that it's OK because I was at the library or doing something else important. And I know that eventually they will get used to the idea.

I am not the first one in my family to face difficulties trying to open up their traditional thinking. My older sisters were the first rebels who fought to Americanize my parents' ways. While fighting for their own rights they also paved the way for the privileges I have now, such as staying out until 8 p.m. and being allowed to go out with friends.

6. **My Sisters' Secret Boyfriends**

My older sisters have taught me a great deal about what my parents expect of me—particularly concerning boys. Although my sisters always understood the value of education, they could not resist having secret boyfriends.

My eldest sister, Jane, had her first boyfriend when she was only 16—not only that, but he was Vietnamese. When my parents found out, the house became a war zone. They resented the idea of a boyfriend, especially one that was not Chinese. Every night the living room was filled with loud arguments in Chinese and never-ending cries. "Stop controlling my life," my sister would scream. "It's not for you to decide."

"If you are under my roof, you'd better listen to me," my parents would yell back. "You shouldn't be distracted from school by boys."

"Fine, I'll move out of the house," my sister said.

My parents had nothing more to threaten her with, except, "You'll never come back under this roof if you're so disobedient. We're not paying for your college tuition."

7. **Focusing on Education**

And Jane did move out with luggage left and right, not caring either about school or about her college education. Eventually, Jane broke away from her Vietnamese boyfriend and made up

REAL STORIES, REAL TEENS

with my parents, but she never did go to college and now works as a beautician.

Jane's experience established the idea that my other sister and I could not have close relationships with guys outside our race. My parents try to divert our attention away from guys by emphasizing the importance of education. It is the goal of many Chinese parents to have children who are highly educated and prominent in society. My parents think that if only my second sister, now a business major, had not also engaged in relationships in high school, she would have entered what they consider a more prominent profession like law or medicine.

They have accepted my interest in science and medicine and want me to be a doctor. Luckily, that's my goal as well, so I probably won't cause family disturbance in that area. If I decide to pursue other areas like interior decorating or broadcast journalism, however, I am sure my parents would object.

8. 'My Friends Can Do Whatever They Want'

Meanwhile, my parents urge us all to retain the customs, language and beliefs of our culture. Last Halloween when I came home from school with neon pink hair, my mom was outraged. "You're looking like one of those gangsters," she said.

"But it's temporary," I told her. "It'll wash off easily in water."

"You'd better not put anything else in your hair again," was all she said after she finished personally washing the dye out of my hair. To my mother, and probably for many other traditional parents too, hair color should be natural—in the case of the Chinese, dark brown or black.

I was furious at how closed-minded my mom was. "Ma," I said, "my friends could do whatever they want to their hair and their parents don't mind."

She glared at me and said, "I don't care what those parents think. Just don't be like them."

As much as I would like to dye my hair, stay out late, not

worry about school and have boyfriends the way my American friends do, I understand that there are valid reasons to follow many aspects of the Chinese culture.

9. Learning to Respect Their Point of View

While the more American side of me becomes angry at the thought of only being allowed to marry another Chinese person, my Chinese side is learning to respect this restriction.

In the past I might have thought that my parents were only trying to be cruel, but I now understand their reasons. Since they only speak minimal English, in order to have a healthy relationship with their sons- or daughters-in-law, it is logical that they should be able to communicate with them. More importantly, our Chinese culture is already being lost in the United States. Prohibiting interracial marriage is their attempt to hold on to our language and tradition.

10. Having It Both Ways

These days, I accept myself as a Chinese-American, meaning that I follow ways of both cultures. In some ways I am more American, like in the way I dress. And I am the one who chooses who my friends are—whether my parents approve or not. After all, I am 17 and capable of leading my own life. Then in other areas I still accept some of the more traditional ways, such as not marrying outside my race.

> **Life in my family is more about school and grades, not relationships.**

Slowly, my parents and I are making progress in compromising with each other. A week after my mom cut those baggy jeans, for instance, I went out and bought another pair. This time, however, they were a little shorter; my parents did not complain about it, and I did not mind the jeans the way they were. My parents can regulate my life to an extent for now, but ultimately I know I will be the one to decide.

The Man in the Glass

By Jessica F.

1.　　Looking through my family album one thing you will notice is that there's a beer can or a bottle in practically every photo. There's one of my father holding me when I was an infant. In his other hand he's holding a can of beer. In another one, my grandfather is sitting in his favorite chair with a bottle of Bacardi rum by his side.

There's one with me and my dad on the ferry boat going to the Statue of Liberty when I was 6. Again there's that familiar can of beer in his hand.

Throughout my childhood my father always put liquor first. I liked to go to parks and the movies with him but he was always hanging out with his buddies in the bars. When he did come to see me he always said, "I ain't got no money. I'm broke." I'd look in his wallet and see that he was putting extra money aside for drinking.

My father rarely treated me with love. He would get aggravated easily and lash out. He had little patience. He would curse at me and tell me to get out of his face. Once I asked him to come to parents' night and he said, "I don't want to go to that BS. Leave me the hell alone."

I tried to talk to him about his problem but he only denied it. I would tell him, "Dad, you're drinking too much. Stop drinking. It's bad for you, you hardly have no money." I would beg him to just try, but he refused.

2.　## A Family Tradition

"Stop nagging," he'd say. "You sound just like your mother." Sometimes I would get so frustrated that I would yell, "Do you want

138

to die like your father?"

My grandfather died from a heart attack when I was very young. I remember seeing him every day in his chair with a bottle of vodka on the table right beside him. Now my father was becoming just like him. He would sit in that same lounge chair in front of the TV, drinking beer. My worst fear was that he would die like his father and leave me all alone.

I couldn't understand why he drank. He had a job, a home, and a family that cared. He didn't need to drink but I couldn't make him see that. There were times when he would tell me that I was the reason he drank. At night I would cry myself to sleep, desperately wanting to believe it, just so I could know that there was some reason.

After a while I gave up. I stopped fighting with him. I avoided him as much as possible. I just didn't give a damn anymore.

But he only got worse. He'd get up in the morning and grab a bottle of vodka from under his pillow. If he didn't get that first drink his hands would shake so badly he couldn't even hold a cup of coffee. It became too painful to watch.

Throughout my childhood my father always put liquor first.

One time he was drunk on the job and miscounted $1,000. They suspended him for two weeks during the holidays. He spent Christmas drinking and sobbing about how he had no money.

3. **I Wouldn't Let Him Off the Hook**

One night we were sitting in the car and again I told him that he was drinking too much. "Shut up!" he screamed. "I don't want to hear it." He put his trembling hands over his ears but I wouldn't stop talking about how he was losing everything: his family, his friends, and soon it was going to be his job.

Then he said he was tired of living this way. He wanted to kill himself. He collapsed in tears and admitted how his mother and I were the only reason why he lived. "Then tell me why are you killing yourself by drinking?" I asked. "I can't stop," he said. "I'm an alcoholic."

I knew that was the first step to recovery.

A couple days later he found out that his job covers treatment for drug and alcohol abuse. He told me he was going away for one month to straighten himself out. The next morning he was gone before I could say goodbye or good luck.

> **People think if they get rid of the liquor, they get rid of the problem. WRONG!**

He went to a treatment center in Pennsylvania. For the first four days he had to go cold turkey. That's when you get all the alcohol out of your system and your body is craving liquor so badly that it hurts. He had to stay in a cabin away from everyone. They do that because the person gets frustrated, angry and desperate. It must have been horrible for him.

4. **The Recovery Process**

After a week he called to tell me how he was doing. At the medical center he learned that he had a swollen liver and a stomach ulcer and he was treated by a doctor. He said he was going to counseling, support meetings, and physical activity programs. He was eating regularly and learning about his problem.

After two weeks he called asking me to visit the clinic for family week. I was excited about my father's recovery but somehow I didn't believe that he would ever truly stop.

At the clinic I stayed in a house with family members of other patients. I discovered that I wasn't the only one suffering. We had sessions where we learned about the things we were doing unconsciously to support the person's habit.

For example, there are times when we mean to do well but

instead we provoke the person to drink more. People think if they get rid of the liquor, they get rid of the problem. WRONG! Every time I used to take the beer out of the fridge and pour it down the drain, my father would only go buy more.

At the treatment center I got a chance to tell my father how I felt for the first time. They gave me a piece of paper with incomplete sentences and I had to fill in the blanks: "I never understood why you..." or "It makes me angry when you..."

5. Opening Up to Each Other

My father was given the same paper. Then we exchanged papers and sat in a circle and read each other's answers aloud. I found out the one thing that got him upset was when I nagged him. I knew I had just as many faults as him but I also knew that it wasn't my fault that he drank.

Then he read my answers aloud. He read how the one thing that I never understood was why he never showed any love towards me. As he kept reading, you could see he was trying really hard to hold back his tears. His voice was trembling and he managed to say he was sorry, that he never realized the pain he caused. Everyone in the room was crying. I didn't think my answers were going to affect anyone but me and him.

Since that day a year ago, my father has changed. He wakes up, only to struggle not to have a drink. My father tells me he could easily "relapse" and take a drink at any time. He did relapse once. Luckily I was there to confront him and help him face himself and his problem. He received treatment and now is recovering again.

He has taken me out to places on special occasions. We go and visit family for dinner and see movies together.

6. I'm Proud of Him

My being supportive has helped his recovery, but he is really the one who is overcoming his own alcoholism. He attends his support meetings once a week and visits his alcohol counselor every other week.

This past Father's Day I was very proud of him because he had remained sober for almost six months. I gave my father a special gift. It was a poem titled "The Man in the Glass" to place by his night table. It described how an alcoholic goes his whole life cheating himself out of the truth.

I gave it to him to remind him that when he drinks he isn't really fooling anyone else. He's fooling the most important person of all—himself.

When I read the poem it made me wonder how my father could look at himself and live a lie. I pictured his reflection on a glass of liquor, the reflection of a face that told a thousand lies all his life. Now that my father is sober, I hope he will never have to face that man in the glass again.

The Fallen

By Paul Langan

"Martin, do you have anything to say for yourself?" Mr. Gates says to me. I can hear anger in his voice.

He's the superintendent of Bluford High School—a large silver-haired man in his late 60s. His lips are pencil thin, and there are bags under his eyes. Bags from listening to stories like mine.

I know he's going to throw me out of Bluford. I can't blame him. All he knows about me is what he's read in the thick folder on his desk.

I can see the pink suspension notices from my seat. He flips through them like he's leafing through an old phone book. I know the words he's reading. I remember the last letter the school district sent to my mother.

> MARTIN LUNA has on multiple occasions displayed severe behavioral problems in school and on school grounds. He has repeatedly engaged in threatening and hostile confrontations with other students, and he has violated school attendance policies numerous times. Furthermore, given his most recent outburst, it is the opinion of this district that he poses a threat to students and faculty. As a result, the district recommends that MARTIN LUNA be expelled from Bluford High School.

My mother cried when she got the letter. I found it laying on our kitchen counter stained with tear drops that made the ink bleed. I crumpled it up right then, but it didn't matter. The damage was done.

Today's my hearing—my last chance.

"Well?" he says. He's looking at me now. He doesn't even blink.

The auditorium is quiet except for someone coughing as I stand to answer him. I hear my mother sniffle behind me. *I'm so sorry for everything, Ma,* I want to say. I feel guilt clawing at my chest like invisible hands.

"Please don't do this," my mother yells out. "He's a good boy. *Please!*" I turn to see her standing at her seat holding her hands as if she's praying to him. Her nose is running and her voice is trembling. It reminds me of how she was three months ago, the day my little brother died. I close my eyes to push the memories back, but it doesn't work.

"Ms. Luna," Mr. Gates cuts in. "I understand this is difficult for you, but we've already heard what you had to say. Now *please* let your son speak."

My mother sits down, crosses herself, and quietly wipes her eyes. She's never backed down from anything, but this time I know she expects the worst. So do I.

Mr. Gates turns back to me. He closes my folder, drops his pen, and rubs his forehead like he's got a bad headache. I am in trouble. No question about it.

"Mr. Luna, in just two weeks at Bluford High School, you have been in several serious fights. You have cut school, skipped classes, and last Friday in the middle of yet another fight, you struck a teacher. This behavior is unacceptable. Unless there are some extenuating circumstances, I'm afraid we have no choice but to expel you. Now, this hearing is your opportunity to tell your side of the story. Martin, what do you have to say for yourself?"

I look up at him because some of his words escape me. *Extenuating circumstances?* I don't know what they are. But I do know there are reasons why I shoved old Mr. Dooling into a wall, why me and Steve Morris keep fighting, why my anger sometimes explodes like a gunshot.

I never meant for any of it to happen. I know I screwed up, especially when I pushed the teacher. But everything else I did was the best I could do, was the only choice I really had.

There's no way Mr. Gates will ever understand this. His eyes tell me what he thinks—expelling me is the right thing to do. There's no changing his mind. I can see that.

Still, like Vicky said, I gotta try. I take a deep breath and begin telling him the truth, how it started days ago when I stumbled into Bluford a bloody mess...

"Oh my God, Martin," Vicky said as she looked at the cut over my eye. Her mouth was wide open and her hands covered her cheeks. "Who did this to you? Was it Steve?"

I shook my head no. I wished she didn't have to see me this way. I could taste blood in my mouth and knew some was on my face. She deserved to know what happened, but I had no time to explain. Frankie and the rest of my crew were on the road, and someone was about to get hurt. I had to do something. Now.

"I'm fine, Vicky. I'll catch up with you later," I said, but my voice cracked into a nasty whisper. I was dizzy. Too many punches to my head.

"Quick, Martin, inside right now," barked Ms. Spencer, our principal. She led me past Vicky straight to the front office. "The rest of you get back to class. There is nothing to see here."

It was almost time for first lunch period, and a small crowd of students had gathered at the front of the school to see my entrance. They looked at me as if I had just shot someone. *What are you starin' at?* I felt like saying, but I had more important things to worry about.

"Ms. Spencer, I need to speak with someone I know. He's a cop. His name is Nelson Ramirez. I need to speak with him. *Now*," I said. She studied my face carefully, not sure whether to trust me.

I couldn't blame her. Where I come from, you don't talk to cops, and you don't expect them to solve problems. I learned that when Huero, my little brother, was killed. For months, my mother and I waited for the police to do something. All we got from them was an apology and some excuses about workload and too many cases.

But Ramirez was different. He was Chicano like us, a friend of my mom's who grew up in the barrio. He held my mom at my brother's funeral and understood that the day Huero died, part of me died too. Where else could I turn?

"I already called the police, Martin." Ms. Spencer said as I collapsed into the squeaky chair in her office. "I called your mother, too. She's on her way," she added.

My headache was getting worse. The last thing I wanted was my mom to see me this way. But I didn't have time to worry about it.

"Call Ramirez," I repeated, rubbing my swollen jaw. "Here's his phone number. Tell him Martin Luna is looking for him." I handed her the crumpled piece of paper he'd given me over the summer.

"Why him?" Ms. Spencer asked, studying the scrap like it was a fake ID card or something. "If you did something wrong, now is the time to tell me so you won't get in any worse trouble."

I wanted to curse her out right there. Behind her wire-rimmed glasses, she couldn't see nothin'. I wasn't afraid of any punishment she could give me. A suspension? A letter? That ain't nothin' compared to watching your brother die in your arms, seeing his blood drip onto your shoes, feeling his skin turn cool in your hands. And now more blood was about to spill.

"There ain't no worse trouble!" I growled, tired of talking to her. I jumped up and reached for her office phone. But my legs were weak, and the room suddenly felt like waves were rolling through the floor. I leaned against the wall to stop from falling.

"*Martin!*" Ms. Spencer yelled, grabbing me and easing me back into the chair. Her eyes were wide with worry.

"*Please*, Ms. Spencer," I said, pointing to the phone.

"Okay, okay. I'm calling him right now. Just sit down and don't move," she said, nervously dialing the numbers. "But if there is something I can do to protect you and the other students in this school, you need to let me know."

Protect me? Too late for that, I wanted to say. The room was spinning. I grabbed the chair to steady myself. "Just call him."

I knew it would come down to this. I knew it the second I agreed to meet my homeboys in the parking lot outside Bluford. Our crew—Frankie, Chago, Junie, and Jesus—were about to do something we had talked about since Huero died. We were going to get revenge.

After months of searching, we found out who shot my brother—a punk named Hector Maldenado. We'd talked about what we'd do all summer. For a while, I dreamed about it night and day. It was the only thing that pushed the hurt away. The only reason I had to get up in the morning.

Don't get me wrong, I ain't a gangbanger. I've stolen a few things and gotten into some fights, but I never did something serious like this before. But everything changed when Huero died. I snapped like an old rubber band.

Frankie Pacheco knew this. He was the oldest and toughest in our crew. He got us guns and showed us what we needed to know. And for a while I was ready to let it all go down like that.

Pop! Pop! Pop!

Just three shots. A blast of sour gun smoke. The screeching of tires as Frankie's old LeMans pulled away. The same sounds I heard the afternoon Huero died. That would be the end of it.

But I couldn't do it.

In my head, I kept seeing my brother's face, Vicky's eyes, my Mom's tears. And I kept hearing something my English teacher, Mr. Mitchell, said. *You could have a bright future ahead of you. Don't throw it away.*

Call me soft. I don't care. You're not the one who sits at your brother's grave, listens to your mother crying in the dark, and knows what it's like to lose someone. If you were, you'd understand why I couldn't be like the coward who drove down our street and stole my brother's life with a gunshot.

"Yes, this message is for Officer Ramirez," Ms. Spencer said. "This is the principal at Bluford High School. I have Martin Luna here in my office. He seems to have been involved in an altercation and wishes to speak with you. He says it's important."

I put my head in my hands. A message! Where was he? It was the one time I needed to reach him, and he wasn't there.

Call me anytime, he had said when he gave me the number. Yeah, right.

I felt Ms. Spencer watching me. I knew she was wishing I never transferred into her school. But if I'd stayed at Zamora High, I'd be in jail or dead already.

That's why my mom moved out of our old neighborhood, making me start my sophomore year at Bluford High. I was so angry when she told me, I almost punched her. Can you believe that? I hate when I get that way, but Huero's death did that to me.

The move added 45 minutes to her bus ride to Wal-Mart where she worked as a cashier with Nilsa, Frankie's older sister. But she did it—to *save* me. It didn't work.

"Where is he?" a man yelled into the office, shattering my thoughts. "Where's Martin?"

I looked up to see Mr. Mitchell. The throbbing in my skull was worsening by the minute, and the room was fuzzy, like an old TV that isn't tuned in right.

"What happened?" he asked, shaking his head. The other day, he gave me an "A" for an essay I wrote about Huero. I wondered what he'd say if he knew another kid was about to die because I was too scared to talk.

I stared at him, my heart pounding. My hands sweating. The room seemed to spin. Overhead, the bell sounded announcing the beginning of first lunch period. Time was running out like blood from a cut.

"Martin, what is it?"

I knew it would take Frankie at least a half hour to get to Hector's house. It hadn't been that long since we fought. If I acted now, there still was a chance I could do something. But I wasn't ready to rat out my boys. I ain't a snitch.

Up until a month ago, Frankie and I were like brothers. *Family*, he called me and the rest of our crew. I even took a beating to earn that word. That's how we did things.

But then Frankie admitted that the bullet that killed my brother was probably aimed at him. I don't know why I never thought of it before, but it made sense. Frankie was the one with the knife wound, the homie most feared on our block, the tattoo-covered 19-year-old who had enemies everywhere. Of course the bullet was meant for him, not an eight-year-old boy. Not Huero.

The news changed me. It was like I'd been asleep and suddenly woke up. Questions kept popping in my head in the middle of the night, cutting our friendship like a knife. Making me secretly hate him. Why did Huero have to pay for what Frankie did? And why was Frankie free to cruise the 'hood while my brother's lying in the ground?

Frankie wasn't stupid. He knew I was changing. That's why he wanted me to do the shooting this morning. It would make me as guilty as him, and it would mean he'd always have something on me in case I gave him trouble. I'm sure he planned it this way. But he didn't plan on me backing out.

"I'm not doin' it, Frankie. I'm serious," I announced while we were all sitting in his LeMans ready to get Hector. The car got as quiet as a grave.

You should have seen Frankie's face. If it were a gun, I'd be dead right now. I jumped out before anyone could stop me.

Chago, my best friend from back in the day, tried to change my mind. He was worried about what Frankie would do next.

"C'mon, Martin. We're family, man. Brothers," Chago said. "Let's go."

The word stung me. *Family*. It was like a slap in my face. Look what the word did to me—it cost me my brother and was about to turn me into a criminal. That ain't what family is supposed to be. Anyone who says so needs to get their head examined.

"My brother was Huero, Chago," I said. "And he's dead because of something Frankie did. You know it's true. What we are about to do, it ain't family, Chago. It's crazy."

Frankie lost it. His jaw tightened up, and he got this cold look I saw once before when he jumped a kid for talking to his girlfriend. The guy was already on the ground when Frankie's foot smashed into his face with a heavy wet thud. I can still hear the sound. The guy moaned and threw up, and Frankie backed away, acting like he was trying to protect his new steel tipped boots from the mess. Like they were more important than another person.

Frankie was ready to do worse to me when he stepped out of his car. Don't get me wrong. I can handle myself in a fight. But I'm no match for Frankie. His fists pounded into my face and side, knocking me to my knees. That's when he pulled out his gun.

"You can't leave your family, Martin," he said. His nine millimeter was pointed at my face. It was the first time I looked into the barrel of a gun.

All I could think about was the bloody mess I'd be when my mother found me, how she'd cry at my funeral with no sons at her side.

"I can't go no further. Do what you gotta do," I said. I whispered a prayer just in case.

Frankie blinked.

Maybe it was the guilt he had for Huero's death. Maybe it was that he didn't want to shoot me in daylight where a crowd of people could witness it. Or maybe it was because he was shocked that I was willing to die to prove I ain't a killer. I don't know what it was, but Frankie let me go.

"This ain't done," he growled and jumped back into his car.

I believe him.

The clock over Ms. Spencer's desk said 10:38. Frankie and the boys had been on the road for 20 minutes already. There were at least two guns in the car, and the only one who knew their plan was me. I was wasting time.

"C'mon, Martin. It's like I said before. You have a choice. You can end this right now," Mr. Mitchell said, staring at me like I was a puzzle. "We're listening."

I could feel myself zoning out, like there was a fog settling over my brain. All last night, I replayed how this day would go down. When I grabbed my bandana and left to meet Frankie, I knew I had to walk away, that Frankie was gonna come at me like never before. But I figured if I could just escape and get to Bluford, it would all be over.

I was wrong.

Looking at Ms. Spencer's tight jaw and Mr. Mitchell's wide eyes, I knew it was just beginning.

You can read the rest of this story in The Fallen, *by Paul Langan.*

REAL SOON
Taking Control of Your Future

Minnesota Merengue:
A Latina Finds Friendship
on a White Campus

By Kizzy Charles-Guzman

1.   When I announced last year that I was going to attend Carleton College my friends nearly passed out. The school is about 90% white, and it's in Minnesota, where it snows until June. I received all sorts of advice and warnings (and a few words of encouragement).

My favorite was: "Just keep in mind that you're going there to study, not necessarily to make friends. So if they don't want to befriend you because you're Hispanic, don't you mind them. Keep your nose in your books. Know what I'm sayin'?"

I hoped Carleton wouldn't be that bad, and I'm used to interacting and relating to people of different races, but I admit that I was nervous about attending a "white" college.

2. Doomed?

My friends swore that I was doomed. I was concerned too, but not as worried as they were. This may be partly because I have not had the upbringing—or outlook on race—of the average American teenager.

I lived in Venezuela for 15 years before my family moved to New York. My mother is a light-skinned Venezuelan and my father is black, from Trinidad.

In Venezuela, most of my friends were the children of Spanish and Portuguese immigrants and we all attended the same private Catholic school. Unlike my school, my neighborhood had all complexions: black, white and everything in between.

3. Growing Up in Venezuela

Although we are all Hispanic in Venezuela, race is still an issue. Most people are dark-skinned, but in general, the lighter you are, the better your position in society is.

Over there, being light-skinned is considered a sign of prosperity because a lot of immigrants from Spain, Portugal and Italy came to Venezuela and eventually established businesses. In other words, the upper class in Venezuela is usually white.

So in Venezuela, I was aware of race, but it was not a big deal for me.

4. In America, Race Is a Bigger Issue

That all changed when I moved to Brooklyn and I realized that, because of the great race diversity, everything seemed to be turned into a race issue. Most of my friends were either black or Hispanic.

They had been born in the States and, having lived all their lives in poor neighborhoods in Brooklyn, they learned to be aware of the inequality of the races. They often wanted to show me how racist America was.

> **I only thought of being myself, and if people liked me, they would accept me.**

When the college application process came around, I applied mostly to private schools because I needed a scholarship. I didn't pay attention to the schools' minority rates until after I applied. All I knew is that I wanted to go away.

However, by the time I got on the plane to fly to Minnesota, I was convinced that I was going to hell. I had come to expect a bleak place where everyone would be mean to me because I'm black and Hispanic.

5. **Comfortable at College**

During the first day of orientation, I walked into a room with about two hundred students. My first thought was, "Wow, I don't have blue eyes. What do I do now!?"

Walking around campus I noticed how few minority students there really are. Blacks made up less than 7% of the students and Hispanics made up about 5% of them. In some classes I was one of two or three students of color.

I couldn't help but notice how "white" the school was, but everyone was so nice to me that I felt comfortable right away. Everyone in school would always smile and talk to me. The other freshmen were always happy to talk about "how they ended up in Carleton," and invariably, we ended up knowing someone else's life story by the end of the night.

6. **Making Friends of All Races**

It helps that my roommate and I are also really close. My friends are surprised because she is white and loves just about every sport. I, on the other hand, consider exercising a punishment. Still, we get along well.

Not only are the people in the school nice, the people in town are too. Strangers smile at you and say hello when you pass them in the streets. People are willing to help you and give you information and, get this, if you ask them for directions, they will often walk you to where you're going if it's nearby.

When I arrived on campus I never thought about hanging out only with the other students of color, despite having been told that white people wouldn't really want to be my friends. I only thought of being myself, and if people liked me, they would accept me.

But some other minority students have different views and experiences. They don't seem to want to learn from other people. They want to join only culture-related clubs, leave the parties as soon as the DJ plays country or alternative music, and complain often about the lack of minorities on campus.

7. **Learning to Relate**

I do not agree. Maybe because of my background, I see things differently. So I don't stick to one crowd at Carleton. I have a lot of friends of all races. I've joined clubs based on my interests, not on race. I'm even developing a taste for country music.

I don't want to take away from my college experience by being exclusive about the people I become friends with. Instead, I enjoy seeing how people can relate even when they come from different backgrounds.

8. **Crossing the Color Line**

I like that I can see our cultures mixing in small ways, like when I came back from a meeting and there were about nine people hanging out in my room, listening to my salsa tapes, even though six of the people were white.

That night we just talked and joked around and all we listened to was Latin music and some reggae.

I was intrigued that they had chosen my music, so I asked them why they were listening to salsa and they just said, "Because we like it." Later, I felt really stupid that I had asked.

I love Carleton. I'm glad that I get to experience life around white people and students of color. I'm not denying that there is racism in the world. I just think that, especially when we go away to college, we should appreciate all cultures and make an effort to cross barriers.

An Army Life for Me

By Elizabeth Sanchez

1.   Senior year in high school is one of the many wake-up calls you'll get in life. You're becoming an adult. To me, that's one of the scariest things.

It means responsibilities—taking care of yourself, and anyone else that comes along. I think physically and mentally I can make it on my own, but I'm not sure about emotionally. I still feel 10 years old sometimes.

I like feeling like I can just curl up in my mother's arms and nothing, not even the boogeyman, can get to me because she's there to scare him away. When I have a "meltdown," like when I question my life so much that I'm on the verge of dropping out of school and crying for no real reason, she's there to pick me back up and hug me.

I feel she'll always be there for me, but I know that being an adult means having to make decisions without Mommy around. What if I choose the wrong one?

2. People Think I'm Crazy

But as much as I'm scared about taking on adult responsibilities, another part of me is ready for the challenge. I have this determination in me that says I can make it far.

And so I've already made one important decision: I'm joining the Army.

Man, so many people think I'm crazy for doing this. A couple of friends and three of my teachers have tried to discourage me from going. My friends said that meant I'd be killing and I'll only be taking orders all my life. I just let their mouths run, because I made up my mind.

A teacher who I trust so much asked me how, as a "bright young student," I could make a decision like that without thinking twice. It was like an icicle went through my heart. I felt that after all those other times we talked and connected, she just didn't understand me anymore. But I didn't say anything to her. I didn't want to make a big deal about it.

I did think about it a lot, but I didn't think twice about signing the papers. I'd prefer not to be in a combat situation, but if it comes down to that, I think I've got the guts for battle.

3. **Just Like My Brother**

One of the main influences in my decision to join the Army is my brother, Domingo. He joined the military after high school. I was 9 and really looked up to him. I loved seeing my brother when he came home for Christmas in his uniform. He looked so handsome and powerful.

> I'd prefer not to be in a combat situation, but if it comes down to that, I think I've got the guts for battle.

Even though I hate to admit it, I'm just like my brother in that we're both blunt and we don't let anyone walk all over us. And like me, Domingo has always had plenty of determination, but no major goal, no direction.

Joining the Army makes sense to me for so many reasons. I love adventure and I'm not afraid of physical labor. (In fact, I'd like to get in shape.)

4. **I'll Use Army Money For College**

I want to serve my country. Yes, I know about the history of this country, including discrimination against minorities and women not being able to vote. But the United States has moved forward and now gives its people more opportunities. I want to give back for that, and for our country preserving our freedom of speech and the right to be who we want to be.

I want to go to college, just not right after high school. My family's not well off, so I'll need the money that the Army gives toward a college education.

In the meantime, I want to travel the world, learn different cultures and languages. I want to be able to make something of myself, make decisions for myself and be pushed to the limits of my physical and mental abilities. I want some life stories to tell the grandchildren about. And I feel I'll get all that in the Army.

5. **I Feel Restless**

I already have a shipping date: two weeks after I graduate from high school. I signed the forms in August and so did both my parents. I was giddy at first, because I thought, "This is really happening to me!" Then, after two months, that excitement died down.

Now I just feel restless. I want to get past high school already. My brother talks to me on the phone on weekends from his base in Georgia. Recently, he told me that I haven't gotten that "wake-up call" yet.

He predicted, "You'll realize you're a grown-up when it's time for you to go into the Army. It happened to me and it will happen to you, too." And I think I'm ready for it all to come my way.

College Can Be Hell

By Tamecka L. Crawford

1.   Going off to college for the first time can be a scary experience for anyone. But it is especially hard for teens who grow up in foster care, like me. We don't have the support of a parent, and a lot of times we feel as if we're alone in the world. Before I left for Sullivan County Community College in New York State, I started to wonder what college life would be like for me.

Although I wanted so badly to be independent, I still wanted someone there to fall back on. How would I survive all alone in a strange place? Could I make it as a college student? Would I fail or drop out? I worried about people finding out I had lived in a group home and treating me differently or making fun of me. I even wondered if my professors would treat me differently.

2. **First-Day Nerves**

Although I had gone on several college tours and seen the campus of my school before I enrolled, I was still nervous.

When I first started classes, things seemed fine. I had six classes and the workload was manageable. But after a while I met a guy and started spending lots of time with him, skipping classes and not studying. I started having trouble, and my grades dropped tremendously in history and math. But I told myself I had all the time in the world to pull my grades up.

I found myself using the excuse of being in foster care every time I missed a class or failed an exam. A lot of times I would say to myself, "Oh, I'm in a group home. Who cares if I go to class or not, or if I failed an exam or even if I passed one?"

3. **'Group Home Child'**

I felt as if the words "group home child" were hanging over my head. Even though nobody treated me differently, in the back of my mind I felt they were. Like at the bursar's window (the place that handles your bills), I felt that they were hesitant to deal with me because they knew I was in foster care.

My self-esteem was very low my first semester. I sometimes just gave up and didn't care. As a result, I completed my first semester with a 1.0 grade point average (a D average), and ended up on academic probation.

I felt nobody cared for me. And it showed. I felt this way because I didn't have any family support. I kept making the mistake of comparing my life to students who had parents calling often and coming to visit them. They also used to get care packages filled with all sorts of things, including their favorite foods, money and supplies they asked for.

Wanting Family

4. I wanted so badly to have someone care about me like that. I felt neglected and jealous.

> How would I survive all alone in a strange place? Could I make it as a college student?

I remember hearing my roommate talk on the phone with her mother, describing what classes she liked more than others. I wished so badly that could be my mother or somebody who really cared for me. Although I did stay in contact with people from my former group home, it wasn't a substitute for family.

Just before the end of the first semester I realized that I had wasted time feeling sorry for myself and I had to do something about it. I never thought the semester would go so quickly. Like I said before, when you first get to college you think you have all this time, then before you know it, it's over.

Gradually I realized that time was passing me by and nobody

REAL STORIES, REAL TEENS

was going to care for me until I cared for myself. I was so wrapped up in worrying about having people do things for me and care for me that I wasn't taking the time to care for myself.

I got tired of using the fact that I was in foster care as an excuse. I was tired of failing my exams. I was tired of crying. At the same time, I also noticed that the people who I was envying weren't doing so well in their classes either.

5. Tired of Excuses

I finally realized it wasn't because I was in foster care that I was failing my classes. It was because I had been paying too much attention to what people thought of me and how they treated me, and too little attention to my schoolwork. I had to accept the fact that I was in foster care and move on. It wasn't being in foster care holding me back, it was me holding myself back.

> **I finally realized it wasn't because I was in foster care that I was failing my classes.**

It was right after spring break that I decided to wipe my eyes and find ways to start my independent life. The first thing I decided to do was to attend all my classes Monday morning and start pulling my grades up.

In my second semester my grade point average shot up to 3.25. I was studying night and day, especially subjects like history, which I always had problems with. I went to a tutor who worked with me and I also found peer tutors (fellow college students who were good in a particular subject) to help me. In exchange, I'd type a paper for them or make them dinner.

I started letting professors know I was having problems and some of them would meet with me privately to help me. Or if they saw that I was making an effort they would let me know, by saying, "I see that your grades are dropping again. Are you having trouble studying?" Some of them would give me methods or extra material to use.

6. **Help from a Counselor**

My next step was to get counseling. When you're on academic probation you automatically get group counseling. I'd had counseling in the group home, but I never liked it because I felt we were prejudged. But in college I felt it would help to have a one-on-one counselor because I realized I needed help dealing with the transition from the group home to college life.

I had a nice female counselor who listened to me talk about school, my group homes and other things on my mind. At the end of the sessions she would give suggestions on how to deal with my problems. It helped me realize that while I couldn't have the family relationships that I wanted so badly, I could thank God for the people who were taking the time out to help me any way they could.

I also got a part-time job to make some extra money when the group home couldn't help me pay for whatever I needed. I was even able to put some money in the bank for rainy days. Basically, I started trying not to depend on the system too much.

By my third semester in school I was no longer seeking as much support from the agency or my worker. I was trying to make it on my own.

Through counseling, I realized that just because people live with their biological families does not automatically make their lifestyle better than mine. I also realized that in some ways being a foster child was an advantage for me.

7. **Strength from Foster Care**

For example, living in a group home was a big help in adjusting to college life because I had already learned how to live with different people's personalities and attitudes. Also, I had already learned a sense of independence. Just like in a group home, when you're in college you have to do things for yourself and make sure things are getting done to help you.

But one thing that was easier for me about the group home

was that everyone has something in common: our family couldn't or wouldn't take care of us. We all understood that and could talk about it amongst each other. But in college I met people from all sorts of different backgrounds, and sometimes I felt envious of their lifestyles. When other students were planning their spring breaks in Hawaii or Virginia, I was deciding on what movie I was going to see during the break, or whether to go visit a relative or stay in the group home. Sometimes I would just end up at the group home the entire time.

I learned that in order for anything to change, I first must care about myself. Then I'll be able to care about the situation and do what I need to. I'm looking forward to finishing my last semester. My overall grade point average is 3.0, which is great compared to how things were looking the end of my first semester.

Poetry Brought Out the Performer in Me

By Shaniqua Sockwell

1.   When I was younger, I had no real creative outlets. I couldn't dance to save my life, I could sing okay, but not well enough, and any sports that required physical contact were out of the question.

But I always loved reading and writing. When I was little and got lonely, books were always there when I needed them. They were always willing to share their knowledge. The first book I read was *Little Women.* And if I wanted to share what I felt inside, I would pick up my pen and write my feelings down.

At 10 years old I discovered my love of writing and poetry. I began to write because I wanted to express my feelings. I learned how to write poetry by studying the poetry of Robert Frost, Maya Angelou, Langston Hughes and Ntozake Shange.

From there I developed my own style, which is a combination of metaphors and not sugarcoating the subjects I write about. My poems came from my imagination and from things I saw. I would sit and try to come up with little verses. Most of the time they rhymed.

My first poem went like this:

The World Is a Gem

2.   *On the smallest island*
in an oyster shell
there is a pearl
that grows and grows.

It dwells beneath the emerald sea
as green as grass can ever be.

Up above the flowers grow
as fiery red as rubies glow.

And up above in sapphire skies
diamond stars are drifting by.

I wrote this one at age 11. I like comparing things with nature. I also wrote another poem called "Brown-Eyed Susan," in which I compare a flower to a girl.

> **Nothing scared me more than when I decided to read my poems for an audience.**

As I matured, I began to write about deeper issues, like love, child abuse, rape, incest, the destruction of nature, Black men and women being neglected in this country, politics, sex, war and myself. Some of the poems were about personal experiences, but most were fictional. My inspiration came from things I saw in movies, real life, or things I read.

3. My First Reading

Sometimes when I finished a poem, I would be shocked at how strongly I felt about the issues I addressed. But nothing scared me more than when I decided to read my poems out loud before an audience.

When I was a junior in high school, I discovered a small café called the Living Room that holds poetry readings once or twice a month. It was right near my school, so I would pass it on the bus. I was always interested in the poetry readings I heard about in the Village, but I'd often heard the audiences down there were tough, so I didn't think I was ready for that. I thought maybe this crowd would be easier to handle.

So, I went in one day after school and asked about the readings. I was kinda nervous, but what did I have to lose by asking? They told me to call ahead of time to reserve a place on the list.

When the day came, I called and reserved my spot. I can still remember my number: 12. Being the shy person I am, I couldn't believe that I was doing this. But there was no turning back now. I wound up going alone because nobody was free to go with me. The reading was at 8 o'clock.

4. **Like Someone's Living Room**

I arrived at the poetry reading and sat down. The room was small and narrow, but the place was packed. For some strange reason, I hadn't become nervous—yet. But I was feeling a little jittery. Maybe it was because I was the only black person in the room. Or maybe it was because everyone in the room was slightly older than me. But I wasn't going to let the way everyone was staring and whispering get to me. I was there to enjoy myself, read my poetry and have a good time.

As I looked around, I was sort of surprised at how the place looked. The café felt like someone's living room, with antique chairs and tables, and bookcases with lots of books and magazines, and they served every kind of gourmet coffee you could think of. And even the way they served it was cool. Instead of drinking from cups, you drink from bowls. But I just had a hot chocolate.

I had planned to read three poems, but after seeing how many people had shown up, I thought maybe I should just read two, a love poem and a poem about being lonely.

5. **Enjoying Myself**

As the night progressed, I found myself more relaxed and comfortable. The poems that people read were really good. Some were really funny, like one poem a man read that was about looking at your mess in the toilet bowl. And some were sad, like the one a lady read about losing her sister to a disease.

Some made you feel sorry for the person, like one about staying with a man who's cheating on you, and some were just too damn long, like the poem a gay man read about being with his lover, which was four or five pages long!

But all in all, I was enjoying myself and nothing was going wrong. I was anticipating my turn and the crowd was nothing like I thought it was going to be. They were pretty supportive. I didn't have a care in the world until...

I walked away from the corner I'd been hiding in all night and got ready for my big moment.

I heard them call my name. Now it was time to get nervous! My palms were feeling sweaty, and I actually started shaking! But I couldn't back out now. So I walked away from the corner I'd been hiding in all night, and got ready for my big moment.

I walked up to the front of the room and went to the mike. The guy had to adjust it for me since I'm short, and when I pulled the mike from the stand, I hit myself in the mouth with it. So I tried to cover up my clumsiness by cracking a joke. I said, "Don't you wish these things came in sizes?" It was corny, but the crowd burst out laughing, which relaxed me.

6. Applause and Compliments

I smiled back at everyone and said, "Hi, my name's Shaniqua, and I'd like to read everyone a couple of poems. Is that cool with you?"

The crowd said yeah, so I began to read. One poem I read was called, "In My Heart You Shall Forever Remain," about two lovers having to leave each other, and the next was called "A Cry in the Night," about a young girl being physically abused.

As I read, I felt my nervousness gradually fading. I continued to read with no worries whatsoever. When I finished, the crowd applauded. I was so happy that I'd done such a good job. People came up to me to compliment me. I felt so good I decided to continue doing the readings.

Eventually I moved on to other places. I now perform at the Brooklyn Moon Café on Friday nights.

7. **Rap-Style Poetry**

The environment there is really nice. The people are open and friendly. A lot of their poems are read out in rap style or they're very cosmic, and a lot of them deal with having to go back to the African motherland. There are a lot of black people there, but sometimes there's a mixed audience. There are paintings and sketches on the walls that you can buy, and instead of clapping when a performer's done, you snap your fingers. I like it a lot and now that I've performed before, I no longer get nervous in front of big crowds. I'm far more relaxed, and I take it all in stride.

A lot of people don't share their talents with everyone. They keep them bottled up because they feel they aren't any good. I know how they feel because that's how I felt about my writing and my poetry. But I finally decided that it was time that I came out of my shell and showed everyone what I was made of.

Performing in front of an audience is as important to me as writing poetry because there's nothing like hearing someone applaud and give you a standing ovation after hearing something you've created. It's a real thrill, and I get a lot of satisfaction from it.

I still haven't made it to the Village yet, but I will. Writing will always be my first love, and I will continue to write so that I can get even better. I dream of winning a Pulitzer Prize, or becoming a bestselling author, and being able to finally say that I've become everything I've aspired to be. I haven't gotten there yet, but ya gotta start somewhere.

My Father's Dream or Mine?

By Desiree Bailey

1.   "You want to be a what?"

My dad looked at me like I had four eyes.

"An anthropologist," I said. "It's perfect for me. Cultures, languages, traveling and..."

"Wait, wait, wait. What about a doctor? A lawyer? You want to dig around in the dirt and look for bones?"

His face was a picture of pure perplexity.

"Actually, that's an archaeologist," I said. "Anthropologists study humans. They study different societies and what divides and binds us."

"Listen, I don't want to tell you what to do but these types of professions don't make money. Fields like medicine and law will always make money because they will always be needed. You have to be where the money is."

What was my dad saying? This was the first time he'd ever really disagreed with my choices, and it was confusing me. What was wrong with being an anthropologist?

It's not like I wanted to run away to join the circus. Being an anthropologist seemed perfect for me. It took all of the things that I loved about life and people and rolled them into one interesting career.

2. ## Questioning My Choices

I'd always thought my dad understood me. Our similarities—like our shared love for music and art—had led me to believe that we were almost the same person. Now he was telling me that my goals for the future weren't good enough and that all I should be concerned about was making money. For reasons that I couldn't quite grasp, I felt betrayed.

Our conversation also stirred feelings of doubt within me. Before talking with my dad, I'd been so sure of what I wanted to do and who I wanted to be. I'd travel the world, sampling cultures, and then settle down to teach at a university when I wanted to start a family. I'd had it all planned out until that moment.

Now I felt like scratching these ideas out of my mind. Was my dad right? Come to think of it, I'd never heard anyone say, "Ooh, I really want to be an anthropologist." Many of my friends want to be something prestigious, like a doctor or a lawyer. Besides, if I worked so hard in high school and college, would I be throwing it away by pursuing a career that didn't pay much?

Desperately, I began to think of what else I could be. When I considered being a psychologist, my dad shot that idea down too.

"It's very competitive and very few psychologists get paid a lot," he said.

Ugh. What was his obsession with money? It was driving me insane. I continued my hunt for a new career, but nothing struck me like being an anthropologist. What was I going to do?

What was wrong with being an anthropologist?

3. Pressure to Decide My Future

I pictured myself being a penniless writer trying to hustle handwritten pieces of my work on a train. OK, maybe that was a little dramatic but I couldn't help being concerned. As a high school junior, with college just around the corner, I felt like I needed to think of something. Quick.

I didn't always want to be an anthropologist. Most 4-year-olds don't aspire to be things that they can't spell. Naturally, since both my parents were nurses, I wanted to become a nurse. But after discovering at age 6 that I loved to put words together, I wanted to become a writer. I remember writing and illustrating tiny loose-leaf books with my cousin in the 1st grade and selling them to our friends for a quarter.

While I never quite gave up my bohemian writing dreams, my career goals started to shift to law when I was 10. The lawyers on TV shows like *The Practice* seemed to be having a great time calling, "Objection!" and besides, everyone "oohed and ahhed" when I said that's what I wanted to be.

Soon enough, however, I realized law was not for me. Lawyers have the power to directly influence the fate of another person and I didn't like that idea. If anything happened to my clients, I thought it would be my fault. After toying with the idea of psychology and writing, I declared myself utterly confused.

4. **The Thrill of Exploration**

Around the 7th grade, all that changed. I began watching documentaries by anthropologists about people in distant places. I was fascinated by the cultures untainted by Western civilization, hidden in the mountains of Nepal or the grasslands of Africa. I was awestruck by languages rolling off foreign tongues, forming words unfamiliar to me but telling stories that I already knew.

I needed to be there. I needed to be surrounded by ancient chanting lit by moonlight. I needed to taste foods that had fed entire tribes for thousands of years. I yearned for the authenticity and truth of these peoples that I didn't know. I had finally figured it out. I was going to become an anthropologist.

I thought I had my future mapped out. Living in a household with two parents and a steady income, money had never been my concern. I wanted to make enough to be comfortable, but I never aspired to be rolling in money. My family didn't seem to worry about money either. That's why it was such a surprise when my dad told me to choose a career with a high salary.

5. **My Parents' Dream**

Maybe I shouldn't have been surprised by his reaction. About nine years ago my family emigrated from Trinidad, an island in the West Indies, to the United States. When we lived in Trinidad, we were not struggling or in the midst of political uprisings, unlike many immigrants from other countries. I had a peaceful, normal childhood until we left when I was 7. The sole reason my family moved to the United States was that golden word: opportunity.

My parents saw that my brother and I had the potential and the drive to rise much higher than they had. It was almost like a silent compromise. We were leaving our comfortable island on a single hope—that my brother and I would make it.

Knowing that my parents had brought me to America for success and later hearing my dad's words about money and career choices, I began to feel as if choosing a profession simply because I liked it was selfish.

"What about the dreams and sacrifices of my parents?" I thought. "Maybe I should forget my aspirations and do something that makes them happy. I should have a career that makes a lot of money. This way, I will be successful and make them proud. All their struggles to rewrite their lives in this strange new country will not be in vain."

> **I thought I had my future mapped out.**

6. Money vs. Happiness

My mind was twisting and turning among the possible paths to take and their probable outcomes.

"Should I choose a decent career that I love and have an average salary?" I wondered. "Or should I strip myself of love and passion and have the six-figure salary? Could I have a career that I love that also pays a lot? And even if I did, would I have enough time to raise and nurture a family?"

All these questions kept swirling and colliding in my mind. Not one of them produced an answer.

Two summers ago, to my dismay, my brother's departure for

the University of Chicago drew the issue of money into our home. My parents were constantly having financial discussions about what they would contribute and how much my brother would take out in loans. I felt that I needed to make a decision about my future soon.

My brother, who is now 19, became a biology major and pre-med student, just what my parents wanted. I was surprised when he told me he was doing this, because he'd told me many times that he wanted to have a career in foreign diplomacy. Had my dad gotten to him too? Though it's possible that he had convinced my brother to study medicine, I decided that my brother simply had a change of heart. I have never known him to do anything that he wasn't passionate about.

> I'm no longer concerned with making a fortune off of my career but I also don't disregard money completely.

7. Looking for Answers

With all the chaos bubbling over in my mind, I decided to pay a visit to my school's guidance counselor, Adriana Vega-Saponara. She is a lighthearted and spirited woman who all the students love to talk to. She welcomed me and asked me what was on my mind.

"I want to become an anthropologist but my dad wants me to choose a career that would make more money," I said.

"My dad told me not to be a teacher because it would not pay much money, but becoming a teacher was the best thing I ever did," she said. "If you choose a job just for money, you may not be happy."

Ms. Vega-Saponara suggested that I volunteer and get internships to obtain a clearer picture about my future. She gave me useful advice about following my heart but still having an education to fall back on. She also told me that in order to choose the right career, I would have to know what I want in life.

8. **Easier Said Than Done**

Even though her advice was reasonable, I had a feeling that it was easier said than done. But our meeting did make me realize that I had endless possibilities and that almost everyone went through this process at this time in their life.

I also knew that I couldn't run around trying to please everyone forever. No matter how much advice I received, my confusion would remain until I was ready to clarify it myself. Something simply had to make sense within me.

I finally decided to talk to my parents about my feelings. My father's responses didn't surprise me. He said he prefers that his children have careers in the medical profession or legal profession. It seemed like his definition of success was earning lots of money.

But my mother's responses caught me off guard.

"I just want you to go to college, gain higher education and choose a job that you feel comfortable with," she said.

When I asked her what she would prefer me to do, she said, "I wouldn't make that decision. Never. That's your individual choice. That's a call you have to make."

Talking to my mom gave me the support I was looking for. I felt relieved that she didn't have the same ideas as my father. She viewed success as having a healthy physical, social, mental and spiritual well-being.

9. **A Sense of Clarity**

Although my dad's responses were expected, my conversation with him also gave me a sense of clarity. I understood why he thought the way he did. His family didn't have much money when he was a child. So he focused on making enough so his family could live comfortably.

During our conversation, he admitted that he became a nurse for the sole purpose of making money. The reasons behind my parents' goals for me became clearer. I began to understand both my mother *and* my father, and in understanding them, I began to understand me.

I still feel obligated to have a decent-paying job, but now I also feel like my mother's support gives me the freedom to do what will make me happy.

10. A Happy Balance

I still want to be an anthropologist but now I know that decision is far from final. I'm young and I have my whole future ahead of me. Even within anthropology, there are so many roads I can take. I'm no longer concerned with making a fortune off of my career but I also don't disregard money completely. I've found a happy medium between the two extremes.

For me to enjoy my life, I have to do what I want to do. And despite my dad's preferences, I know that he'll be proud of me even if I don't do exactly what he wants.

So even though I don't have my future mapped out to the minute, I no longer feel plagued by feelings of confusion. I'm secure enough in myself to not have all the answers yet. Wherever life takes me, I will strive to be a success in my own eyes.

Credits

The stories in this book originally appeared in the following publications by Youth Communication:

"My School Is Like A Family," by T. Shawn Welcome, *New Youth Connections*, May/June, 1994

"Bonding Through Cooking," by Aurora Breville, *Represent*, November/December, 1995

"When Politics Gets Personal," by Jason Montoya, *New Youth Connections*, September/October, 2004

"Can a Teacher Be a Friend?" by Zeena Bhattacharya, *New Youth Connections*, March, 1994

"Running From Myself," by Jennifer R., *New Youth Connections*, November, 2002

"A Short Cut to Independence," by Anita Chikkatur, *New Youth Connections*, September/October, 1994

"I'm Black, He's Puerto Rican. So What?" by Artiqua Steed, *New Youth Connections*, January/February, 1996

"I've Been an Adult Too Long," by Marlene Peralta, *New Youth Connections*, January/February, 1999

"Princess Oreo Speaks Out," by Dwan "Telly" Carter, *New Youth Connections*, January/February, 2004

"The Fantastic Four," by Stephen Simpson, *New Youth Connections*, January/February, 1999

"The Crew from the Parking Lot," by Ferentz Lafargue, *New Youth Connections*, November, 1992

"Girl, Stop Fronting!" by Chantel Clark, *Represent*, November/December, 2002

"My Boy Had a Boyfriend," by Odé A. Manderson, *New Youth Connections*, May/June, 2000

"A Sad Silence," by Desirée Guéry, *New Youth Connections*, November, 2002

"My Father: Guilty or Innocent?" by T. Shawn Welcome, *New Youth Connections*, May/June, 1994

"Just the Two of Us," by Stephen Simpson, *New Youth Connections*, December, 1998

"Learning to Forgive," by Christopher B., *Represent*, March/April, 1996

"My Secret Addiction," by Christina G., *New Youth Connections*, November, 1997

"I Could Have Been Elisa," by James Knight, *Represent*, January/February, 1996

"Chinese Parents, American Me," by Ngan-Fong Huang, *New Youth Connections*, April, 1997

"The Man in the Glass," by Jessica F., *New Youth Connections*, March, 2005

"Minnesota Merengue," by Kizzy Charles-Guzman, *New Youth Connections*, January/February, 1999

"An Army Life for Me," by Elizabeth Sanchez, *New Youth Connections*, November, 2002

"College Can Be Hell," by Tamecka L. Crawford, *Represent*, September/October, 1995

"Poetry Brought Out the Performer in Me," by Shaniqua Sockwell, *Represent*, May/June, 1996

"My Father's Dream or Mine?" by Desiree Bailey, *New Youth Connections*, December, 2005

About Youth Communication

Youth Communication, founded in 1980, is a nonprofit youth development program located in New York City, whose mission is to teach writing, journalism and leadership skills, and to make youth voices heard as widely as possible. Each year, 100 public high school students write and illustrate Youth Communication's two award-winning teen magazines. The writers are a diverse group, including teens in foster care, recent immigrants and low-income youth. Working with full-time professional editors, the writers may take several months to complete a single story. This process results in writing of uncommon depth and authenticity. The true stories in this anthology were written by teens in the Youth Communication writing program.

In addition to publishing magazines, Youth Communication has published more than 70 anthologies on topics teens consider most important, such as peer pressure, families, and improving their communities. Stories by teens at Youth Communication are also frequently reprinted in popular and professional magazines, from *Cosmo Girl* to the *Harvard Educational Review.*

Youth Communication strives to serve three primary audiences: teen writers, teen readers and educators.

• Writers: Writing for peers motivates teens to develop their literacy skills, meet deadlines, take individual responsibility and work as a team to produce high-quality magazines.

• Readers: Teen readers report that reading their peers' stories makes them feel less isolated and more hopeful about the future. They also say that the stories give them information they can't get anywhere else and promote discussions with parents and other significant adults.

• Educators: Teachers and youth workers use Youth Communication publications to inspire reluctant readers and to broach difficult topics in safe and stimulating ways. They also report that reading our books and magazines show them what's really important to teens, which helps them establish better relations with their students and clients.

Youth Communication®
224 W. 29th St., 2nd fl.
New York, NY 10001
212-279-0708
www.youthcomm.org

About Development Without Limits

The mission of Development Without Limits is to provide dynamic and challenging learning experiences for young people and adults. Development Without Limits works with community-based organizations, after school and summer programs, schools and other educational institutions in developing curriculum and training staff.

The philosophy of Development Without Limits is based on the idea that people learn best and are most productive when they are interested and engaged in what they are doing, and when learning itself feels meaningful. For this kind of engagement to occur, activities need to be dynamic and based upon the skills, interests and ideas of the participants. This means that we approach each project as something new, tailoring programs, curriculum and staff development to meet the unique needs of each organization.

Development Without Limits can provide training in how to implement the Real Stories program in your school or out-of-school setting.

Development Without Limits
16 W. 32nd St.
New York, NY 10001
212-244-4351
www.developmentwithoutlimits.org

About Townsend Press

Townsend Press (TP) is an educational publisher of an acclaimed series of reading, vocabulary and writing textbooks for the school and college markets. TP also publishes, through their nonprofit foundation, an affordable library of original and classic paperbacks.

The mission at TP is twofold. First, TP strives to create high-quality, reasonably-priced textbooks that help students learn the language skills needed for success. Second, TP seeks to promote reading by publishing a library of compelling $1 paperbacks, sponsoring scholarship contests, distributing reading motivation posters and donating books to schools and community organizations.

The Bluford Series is a collection of 13 young adult novels that focus on the lives of a group of high school students and their families. The series draws its name from the school which many of the characters attend: Bluford High, named after Guion "Guy" Bluford, America's first black astronaut.

Set in contemporary urban America, each novel addresses complex topics relevant to the lives of today's students: family, friendship, trust, isolation, violence and peer pressure, to name a few.

In addition, the books feature male and female characters and include elements from many literary genres, such as mystery, suspense, romance and a touch of the supernatural. In other words, the Bluford Series offers something for almost every reader.

Finally, the books are short (less than 200 pages) and written in a highly readable style. Reviewed in a national reading journal and praised by students and teachers nationwide, the Bluford Series appeals to readers of all ages.

To order the Bluford Series and other books by Townsend Press, go to www.townsendpress.com.

Townsend Press
439 Kelley Drive
West Berlin, NJ 08091
800-772-6410
www.townsendpress.com

Acknowledgments

Youth Communication would like to thank Anita Strauss of the Queens Community House, and Zola Bruce and John Kixmiller of the Center for Family Life in Sunset Park for helping to set up the workshops in which many of these lessons were developed and tested. Irene Shen and Joi Kohlhagen co-taught many of the classes with Keith Hefner and provided valuable feedback.

Many foundations supported this work. The Altman Foundation and the Robert Bowne Foundation provided direct support to our after school curriculum development efforts. In addition, our work with teens at Youth Communication to develop on the stories in the Reader was supported by grants from the Annenberg Foundation, the Clark Foundation, the Cricket Island Foundation, the Charles Hayden Foundation, the Open Society Institute, the Pinkerton Foundation, the Spunk Foundation, the W. Clement & Jessie B. Stone Foundation, the Surdna Foundation, and the Vivendi/Universal Foundation.

Development Without Limits would like to acknowledge lead writers Eric Gurna, Andrea Kamins and Lissette Resto-Brooks, and editor Nancy Linnon.

Thanks to the Developmental Studies Center, the Partnership for After School Education (especially Janet Kelley) and The After School Corporation (especially Stefan Zucker and Kim Baranowski) for their pioneering support of quality after school programming.

The contributing editors, listed on the copyright page, ran the Youth Communication teen writing workshops and edited the stories that appear in *Real Stories, Real Teens*.

The Real Stories Program

Real Stories is a youth development and reading program created for use in out-of-school time settings like after school and summer programs. It is also suitable for informal school settings, like advisories. It is aimed at middle and high school students. The Real Stories program consists of this anthology and an extensive *Leader's Guide*.

Reading the stories in this book, talking about them with peers, and engaging in the activities from *The Leader's Guide to Real Stories, Real Teens* helps young people explore ideas and values, engage in healthy discussion, and form deeper relationships with peers and adults.

In many of the stories, the writers describe how they coped with significant challenges. The activities in the *Leader's Guide* help teens imagine how they would manage similar challenges (or avoid them in the first place). They also show teens how they can be helpful and supportive of their peers.

A key benefit of the Real Stories program is that it makes reading an enriching and rewarding experience. Though Real Stories is not a traditional reading program, it will help increase young people's skills and motivation to read because the activities are based on reading stories that teens will enjoy.

How It Works

Real Stories uses essays written by teens and excerpts from young adult literature to stimulate experiential learning and discussion. The sessions in the *Leader's Guide* are based on a workshop model. Each workshop focuses on a theme and has four parts:

1) An opening activity from *The Leader's Guide* to introduce the theme;

2) Reading a true story by a teen (or an excerpt from a young adult novel) with facilitated discussion;

3) An experiential learning activity that helps participants connect the themes in the story to their own lives;

4) A closing reflection.

The activities that accompany the young adult novel excerpts are structured the same way as the activities for the true stories by teens, with experiential activities and reflection. The goal is to introduce fiction—and to whet the teens' appetites for reading an entire book—without making the lessons seem school-like.

About the Writers

The Teen Writers: The true stories in *Real Stories, Real Teens* were written by teens in Youth Communication's intensive writing workshops. Teens participate in the workshops to improve their skills, learn about themselves, and write stories that will benefit their peers and the adults who work with them. Today, many of these young writers are continuing to make important contributions to their communities. Several of them have gone on to become teachers, principals, police officers, environmental activists and college professors.

Keith Hefner is the executive director of Youth Communication, which he co-founded in 1980. In addition to directing Youth Communication's youth development programs, he has been a Revson Felllow at Columbia University and is the recipient of a MacArthur Fellowship and the Luther P. Jackson Excellence in Education Award from the New York Association of Black Journalists.

Also By
Youth Comunication

The Struggle to Be Strong: True Stories by Teens About Overcoming Tough Times. Foreword by Veronica Chambers. Help young people identify and build on their own strengths with lessons by using 30 personal stories about resiliency. (Free Spirit)

Starting With "I": Personal Stories by Teenagers. "Who am I and who do I want to become?" Thirty-five stories examine this question through the lens of race, ethnicity, gender, sexuality, family, and more. Increase this book's value with the Free Teacher's Guide, available from youthcomm.org. (Youth Communication)

In Too Deep: Teens Write About Gangs. These teens write candidly about the impact of gang violence on their lives and community, including friends who were murdered. Some describe how they left gangs and turned their lives around. (Youth Communication)

The Courage to Be Yourself: True Stories by Teens About Cliques, Conflicts, and Overcoming Peer Pressure. In 26 first-person stories, teens write about their lives with searing honesty. These stories will inspire young readers to reflect on their own lives, work through their problems, and help them discover who they really are. (Free Spirit)

Out With It: Gay and Straight Teens Write About Homosexuality. Break stereotypes and provide support with this unflinching look at gay life from a teen's perspective. With a focus on urban youth, this book also includes several heterosexual teens' transformative experiences with gay peers. (Youth Communication)

190

Things Get Hectic: Teens Write About the Violence That Surrounds Them. Violence is commonplace in many teens' lives, be it bullying, gangs, dating, or family relationships. Hear the experiences of victims, perpetrators, and witnesses through more than 50 real-world stories. (Youth Communication)

From Dropout to Achiever: Teen Write About School. Help teens overcome the challenges of graduating or getting a GED which may involve overcoming family problems, bouncing back from a bad semester, or dropping out for a time. These teens show how they achieve academic success. (Youth Communication)

My Secret Addiction: Teens Write About Cutting. These true accounts of cutting, or self-mutilation, offer a window into the personal and family situations that lead to this secret habit, and show how self-awareness can help get this problem under control. (Youth Communication)

Sticks and Stones: Teens Write About Bullying. Shed light on bullying, as told from the perspectives of the perpetrator, the victim, and the witness. These stories show why bullying occurs, the harm it causes, and how it might be prevented. (Youth Communication)

Boys to Men: Teens Write About Becoming a Man. The young men in this book write about their confusion, ideals, and the challenges of becoming a man. Their honesty and courage make them role models for teens who are bombarded with contradictory messages about what it means to be a man. (Youth Communication)

Through Thick and Thin: Teens Write About Obesity, Eating Disorders and Self Image. Help teens who struggle with obesity, eating disorders and body weight issues. These stories show the pressures teens face when they are confronted by unrealistic standards for physical appearance, and how emotions can affect the way we eat. (Youth Communication)

To order these and other books, go to:
www.youthcomm.org
or call 212-279-0708 x115

CPSIA information can be obtained at www.ICGtesting.com
Printed in the USA
267713BV00005B/1/P

9 781933 939704